Seasoned
by the Sea

We dedicate this book to our parents,
Jean and Vernon Amos,
who reside in Cape Breton, Nova Scotia,
and
Louise and (the late) Joseph Ahern.
All four of them have been un-ending sources of support and love for us.

SEASONED

by the SEA

Delicious fish from the waters off
Cape Cod, Nantucket & Martha's Vineyard

◆

BY CYNTHIA & ROBERT AHERN

◆

THE PENINSULA PRESS
CAPE COD

Design by Betsy Roscoe Morin.
Cover photograph by Patrick Wiseman.
Table setting presented on cover courtesy of
The Nantucket Trading Company
Hyannis, MA

Published by
The Peninsula Press · Post Office Box 644 · Cape Cod 02670 USA
Donald W. Davidson,
Publisher

First published in 1994 by The Peninsula Press.

Library of Congress Catalog Card Number: 94-066787
Ahern, Cynthia & Robert.
    Seasoned by the Sea: Delicious Fish from the Waters off Cape Cod, Nantucket & Martha's
Vineyard
        The Peninsula Press, ©1994.
        Includes index and illustrations.
ISBN 1-883684-04-8
1. Cape Cod, Nantucket & Martha's Vineyard -- Seafood.
2. Cape Cod, Nantucket & Martha's Vineyard -- Cooking.
3. Cape Cod, Nantucket & Martha's Vineyard -- Fisheries.

First edition
Manufactured entirely on Cape Cod in the United States of America
1 2 3 4 5 6 7 8 9 / 02 01 00 99 98 97 96 95 94

Foreword

    7

The Offshore Catch

    8

The Spring Catch

    15

Spring Recipes

Gourmet Pizza with White Clam Sauce
Dairy-Free Clam Chowder
Sole Oscar ❖ Flounder Florentine with Cream Sauce
Mackerel en Papillote ❖ Salmon in Filo with Scallion Remoulade
Mackerel with Sesame-Dijon Glaze ❖ Smoked Salmon Primavera
Squid Bolognase ❖ Shrimp & Clams with Linguine
Shad Roe ❖ Linguine with White Clam Sauce
Scrod San Sebastian

    20

The Summer Catch

    36

A Summer Menu

Mussels Diablo ❖ Crabmeat Cocktail with Dijon Sauce
Crabmeat Spread on Toast Rounds ❖ Marinated Mussels
Key West Conch Chowder
Seafood Pasta Salad ❖ Calamari Salad
Chilled Poached Halibut with Dijon Sauce
Oriental Steamed Salmon ❖ Blackened Salmon
Striped Bass in Filo with Red Pepper Mayonnaise
Grilled Swordfish ❖ Seafood en Brochette
Grilled Yellowfin Tuna with Tomato Mint Sauce
Grilled Fresh Tuna with Rosemary Lime Marinade
Grilled Striped Bass with Fresh Fruit Salsa
Mako Shark Steak au Poivre

    42

The Autumn Catch

    62

An Autumn Menu

Smoked Bluefish Paté
Broiled Oysters on the Half Shell ❖ Oysters Rockefeller
Cape Scallop Appetizer
Creamy Oyster & Spinach Stew ❖ Cape Scallop Stew

Table of Contents

Mussels Steamed with Garlic & Wine ❖ Broiled Cape Scallops
Flounder Pinwheels with Mushroom Marsala Sauce
Mussels Palermo ❖ Baked Fish with Pesto
Lobster Pie ❖ Sole Almondine

66

The Winter Catch

80

A Winter Menu

Portuguese Stuffed Mussels
Shrimp & Artichoke Hearts Wrapped with Bacon
Crabmeat Patrice ❖ Terry's Clams Casino
Smoked Salmon & Caviar Pizza
Spicy Seafood Stew ❖ New England Fish Chowder
Scrod Oreganata
Baked Fish with Breadcrumbs & Fennel Seeds
Baked Fish with Cheddar Crumbs
Seafood Newburg en Casserole ❖ Sea Scallops Marsala
Mussels Marinara ❖ Sea Scallops Provençal

84

Kitchen Notes

Determining Freshness
Storing Seafood ❖ Freezing Seafood ❖ Defrosting Seafood
Preparing Seafood for Cooking ❖ Skinning Finfish
Cooking Fish ❖ Checking for Doneness
Making Fish Stock
About Mussels
Inspecting Mussels ❖ Cleaning Mussels ❖ Steaming Mussels
Opening Oysters
Peeling Shrimp ❖ Deveining Shrimp
Cleaning Squid

98

Index

106

Acknowledgments

110

It goes without saying that Cape Cod, Nantucket & Martha's Vineyard all have changed greatly over the past three hundred years. Once a full day's journey from Boston, this peninsula and these islands now can be close enough in travel time to be a suburb of that city, complete with many of the same conveniences and inconveniences of the late Twentieth Century.

But if you know where to look, you can still find slices of life that have more connections with the past than to the future. The world of the Cape & Islands fisherman is one of those places, and we are thankful every day that we are able to be connected to that world.

The fishermen with whom we deal every day are still rugged, self-sufficient individuals whose livelihood depends solely upon their ability to understand and survive the elements of nature. Their lives depend upon good judgment and quick-thinking on an unforgiving ocean. The food and shelter that they provide for their families only come if they are successful each day. They receive no unemployment benefits. They get no pay for sick days. They take no paid vacations. Instead, they must go to sea each day and prove their ability anew.

Meanwhile, they exist in every town on the Cape & Islands without a great deal of notice. Their boats range in size from skiffs of only sixteen feet to ships of a hundred feet or more. Their understanding of going to sea and returning with a saleable product has been carried on by generations of their forbearers: Nickersons, Bassetts, Bakers, Richardsons, and the like. They are not always easy to deal with, and they don't always agree with each other, but they *do* know how to fish.

We consider ourselves fortunate to be so connected to this old world amid a rapidly changing new one. We are forever thankful that we know about these people and that they continue to make these daily trips to the sea, then back to the shore so that we are able to sell the fruits of their labors.

This book is dedicated to all of these fishermen, from all of the towns on Cape Cod, Nantucket & Martha's Vineyard. But, in particular, it is dedicated to those from the port of Chatham.

Cecy & Bob Ahern
Chatham, Cape Cod
June, 1994

CECY & BOB AHERN washed ashore on Cape Cod in 1972 and landed in Chatham, where they still live. Fresh out of college with degrees in English and Education, Bob found his part-time work in a fish market of greater use. For several seasons, he managed Swan River Fish Market, while Cecy worked at the Swan River Restaurant. They spent their winters travelling (collecting recipes all the while), commercially fishing, building their home, and raising two handsome sons.

Early on in the 80s, they had the good fortune to become owners of the Swan River Restaurant & Fish Market, which they continue to operate in its original coastal setting today. Though the restaurant remains a seasonal business, the fish market now operates throughout the year and supplies restaurants as far south as Florida with freshly-caught fish from the waters off Cape Cod, Nantucket & Martha's Vineyard.

There is only one place to begin this cookbook about fish from the waters off Cape Cod, Nantucket & Martha's Vineyard, and that is to begin with the Cape's historic namesake, the codfish.

Cod is scrod is schrod is cod. That takes care of the Number One question ever asked in any fish market.

Actually, *scrod* is (please take notes on this) a generic term for a small, white-fleshed, fillet of any number of different fish. By definition, it should be a fish that is small: 1 to 3 pounds when whole. Scrod can be cod, haddock, pollock, hake, or any other North Atlantic whitefish that flourish offshore in Georges Bank. In most fish markets throughout the Cape & Islands and New England, scrod is cod, unless it is otherwise noted, such as *scrod haddock*. Right off the boat, in fact, cod is separated into three classifications: *scrod cod* (1 to 3 pounds each), *market cod* (3½ to 12 pounds each), and *steak cod* (over 12 pounds with their heads off).

From Boston to Boise, most cod found on the market today is caught by draggers or net. The boats used are out to sea for many days at a time. As a result, the fish is banged and bruised to the point that it is lucky to be dead. Often, a week goes by before the cod gets to the plate.

The cod which we receive at the Swan River Fish Market, however, is caught by the oldest method still in commercial use today: hook-fishing. Our cod fishermen use two traditional methods: tub trawling (with many hooks set on floats) and hand-jigging. For centuries, jigging was the only way to catch cod, and it still remains the best. It is very labor intensive, and it yields only about one percent of all the cod on the market today.

Each fisherman uses one line with one hook on it. He can be anywhere from twenty miles to seventy-five miles out to sea in ocean depths of one hundred to six hundred feet. He simply drops his weighted

Cod

hook and bounces it off the bottom until a codfish hits it. Then, in comes the fish, which is immediately cleaned, washed, and iced. Within a few hours, that fisherman has headed back for Cape Cod, Nantucket or Martha's Vineyard. In our case, the fishermen land at Chatham or Harwichport, and the fish is brought to us for filleting the next day. *That* is fresh fish!

Unfortunately, cod is one of many in our local waters that are suffering from overfishing. During the past twenty years, fishing technology has advanced so much that the stocks of many species have been seriously depleted. Each year, I have seen the catches decline and the fishermen land fewer fish. This is certainly not due to the smallboat fishermen based on Cape Cod, Nantucket & Martha's Vineyard.

The huge fleets fishing out of Boston, New Bedford, and Gloucester have become far too efficient with their electronic fish-finders, bottom-scouring dragger nets, and other unimaginable changes in methods that have brought the North Atlantic fish stocks down to perilous levels. If all the fishermen taking cod and haddock were hook-fishing, we would never be in such a situation. Of course, if there were only bicycles, we wouldn't have any automobile accidents either. The real world intrudes.

Federal management plans are underway to limit the amounts of fish that can be taken from our waters. While no one in the industry looks forward to these measures, they must be taken. Fortunately, the plans being discussed may exempt hook fishermen. If so, small fish markets on the Cape & Islands will still be able to buy fresh fish from the local fleet. Quotas on fish caught are probably the best way to ensure that there will always be fish tomorrow. Hook fishing in small boats is another.

Meanwhile, we should appreciate the fact that cod is probably the most versatile of all our fish. It is absolutely delicious when prepared in the most simple of fashions: broiled quickly with a touch of butter, as well as salt and pepper on top. The best way to ruin cod is to cook it too long, and that is easy to do. A one-pound fillet of scrod, which will feed two average eaters, takes only five to eight minutes under the broiler.

There are any number of wonderful tasting offshore finfish closely resembling cod. Most of these are still underutilized and unappreciated (except by gourmet chefs and fishermen's wives!) Cusk, pollock, ocean catfish, and hake, to name a few, are usually available for half the price of haddock and cod. Visitors to our market are always full of questions about these "unknown" species. With great interest, they always ask about them, but then they still purchase haddock or cod. What can I say?

Cusk and ocean catfish both come from the deep, unpolluted waters of Georges Bank, and they are somewhat firmer in texture than pollock

We should appreciate the fact that cod is probably the most versatile of all our fish.

and hake. All of these species are by-catches, caught incidentally, while the fishermen are targeting cod, haddock, or the so-called "flat fish", sole and flounder. These fish all are sold skinless and boneless in fillets that are generally 1 or 2 pounds each and 1½ inches thick.

Any of Cecy's recipes which calls for haddock or scrod could be used with these species as well. Experiment. Buy according to availability. Pick out the freshest fish that day. You won't be disappointed. Not long ago, we ran a special in our restaurant on pan-blackened ocean catfish. Unheard of! Not too be found in any cookbook. (Yet!) But the taste and the response would have brought a smile to the face of any Cajun chef.

Yet another great-tasting fish from our offshore waters is whiting, a small fish, weighing one to one and a half pounds when whole. Too small to fillet, whiting is generally cooked whole. Though it is served with the bone intact, the delicate, white meat flakes easily away from the bone, and the taste is absolutely worth the effort. In fact, you'll find that the flavor and the moisture make whiting one of the tastiest white fish.

One of the most unfortunate things about our American approach to eating fish is our paranoia about bones. In most of the world, fish is sold and cooked whole. I'll never forget the sight in the Mercado in Seville, Spain of fish stall after fish stall with all the fish displayed on ice, *whole!* The fish sold that day were steaked through from one side, but left attached at the bottom so that they could be splayed out like an accordion. As customers bought their steaks, the fishmongers would simply cut the rest of the way through, then bag them up.

The taste of fish cooked with bone and skin still intact really is so much better. Consider the contrast between a dry, baked chicken breast and a chicken roasted whole. Though so much of the flavor comes from the skin and the bone, we just can't seem to convince Americans. Only the Old World and ethnic cooks, whether Chinese, Japanese, Italian, Portuguese, or Greek, seem to appreciate this point!

Whiting was introduced to me by one of the Cape & Islands' most noted fishmongers, Cosmo Montagna. Cozzie has operated a fish market for some thirty years out of the basement of a building he owns in Hyannis. One day I was driving a fish truck with freight for him, and after I delivered the whiting, he asked me if I had ever tasted the fish. "Of course not," I told him. I had been raised on fried haddock on Fridays (or fish sticks if times were bad.) "Well, don't worry about your next stop," he said. "Forget your waiting boss watching the clock. You're going to have a treat." Cozzie took three plump whiting, deftly cleaned out the entrails, floured them well, then fried them. What a taste! A revelation! Cozzie, I'll *always* be indebted to you!

Menu

Appetizer
Gourmet Pizza with White Clam Sauce

Soup
Dairy-Free Clam Chowder

Entrées
Sole Oscar
Flounder Florentine with Cream Sauce
Mackerel en Papillote
Salmon in Filo with Scallion Remoulade
Mackerel with Sesame-Dijon Glaze
Smoked Salmon Primavera
Squid Bolognase
Shrimp & Clams with Linguine
Shad Roe
Linguine with White Clam Sauce
Scrod San Sebastian

SPRING

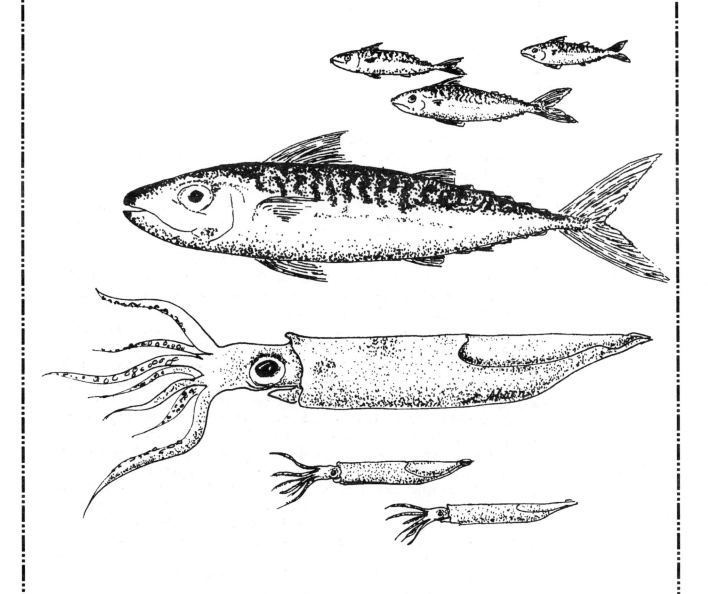

The Spring Catch

The advent of spring should be reason enough for joy throughout Cape Cod, Nantucket & Martha's Vineyard, and it is. In the world of fresh fish, however, spring brings countless other reasons for us to smile. Our fish counter literally fills up with species we could only dream about in the winter. The ocean begins to warm, fish migrate north, clams rise up from their winter depths, fish spawn, the herring run. Changes, anticipated delights, cycles renewed. You've gotta love it!

One of the first signs of spring comes from the lowly herring's aristocratic relative, the shad. Shad roe, the egg sac of the bony shad fish, is a traditional spring meal in the northeast. An acquired taste, to be sure, shad roe tops the list for many a Yankee.

Shortly after the shad roe arrive, our local trap fishermen set out their nets. This ancient form of fishing has died out in most regions. From our market, we can see this fishery still in active and productive use. It involves driving thirty-foot long poles into the sandy bottom from large open wooden boats. Nets are strung between the poles, which funnel migrating fish into a heart-shaped center. There the fish are trapped and live, until the boats bring them the few miles to shore. Nothing could be fresher. These weirs are only productive for two months each spring, but they yield hundreds of thousands of pounds of the highest quality fish.

The first fish caught in these weirs are squid, and the quality of this catch is far superior to any caught by dragger boats. In draggers, squid get tossed and mangled, and they lose their best qualities before they get to the dock. Trap-caught squid are alive and at the dock within an hour or two. The boats unload a couple of miles from our market, so it is then only minutes before they are on ice for our customers!

Truly, one of the most amazing sights to be seen, better than tulips and daffodils popping up in spring, is the sight of a trap fisherman standing waist-deep amidst oozing squid in the middle of his trap boat! It is an unforgettable sight! Picture Captain Paul Lucas, a man of substantial girth, sailing up the Herring River to his dock. The boat's rails are only inches above the water. From stem to stern and across the entire deck, nothing but thousands of pounds of squid and *Captain Eelgrass*. When he needs to move from his wheel he just shifts into the squid and waits for the mass to fill in behind him! Words cannot describe!

The squid are still alive, and during their season the weather is always raw and damp on the waterfront. They are then hauled up onto the dock, loaded into barrels of iced saltwater, and trucked off to market. And *Captain Eelgrass* goes home to Squid Dreams.

Unfortunately, squid season only lasts three or four weeks. We try to freeze a few thousand pounds for use over the summer. In fact, the U. S. Department of Fisheries recommends freezing squid to tenderize it, and the fish loses nothing in quality (which is rare for seafood.)

Our next spring catch in the weir traps is mackerel. Again, the quality of trap mackerel far surpasses that of any other caught. These mackerel actually flush out their stomachs while trapped in these nets. There is no bait for them to eat. And the result is the highest quality fish of the year.

A fresh trap mackerel is lean, delicious, and not at all oily. When properly cooked, this fish will surprise fussy eaters with its mild taste. A wonderful and inexpensive source of both protein and flavor that has long been a valued food source in Europe and elsewhere, mackerel remains one of America's most under-utilized fish resources.

Meanwhile, mackerel make an even shorter appearance in Nantucket and Vineyard Sounds than do squid. Driven out of these waters by that most voracious of predators, the bluefish, the mackerel migrate northward to Cape Cod Bay and the Gulf of Maine for the rest of the summer. Close on their tailfins in huge schools during late spring, the bluefish arrive skinny and hungry from their long trip up from southern waters. They will be found in the sounds and bays throughout the summer, and often they linger until October if the weather stays warm.

Bluefish is another species which suffers from a bad reputation of its oily flavor. If the bluefish is fresh and properly handled, however, nothing could be further from the truth. Too often these fish are caught by sportfishermen, who bring ice for their beer, but not for their fish. Instead, their catch sits uncleaned and abused in the sun for hours. If cleaned and iced on the boat, however, then cooked within a day or two, fresh bluefish is delicious and full of flavor. If you've never done bluefish right, give it a try, and you'll be pleasantly surprised.

The Spring Catch

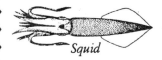
Squid

Spring is also the season for flounder, a family of fish that represents dozens of varieties. Often called *flatfish*, the members of the flounder family are different from other *finfish* simply because they are truly flat instead of round. While they are all hatched with one eye on each side of the head, one eye travels over the top during maturity until it ends up right next to the other. The flatfish then inhabits the very bottom of the river or ocean, often burying itself in the mud and showing only those eyes. The most common flounder we sell include: yellowtail, black-back, dab, and fluke. Sole is another cousin of the flounder. The grey sole is one of our most popular fish; lemon sole is another we sometimes see.

Most of the flounder unloaded in our ports are caught by draggers, local boats that can fish anywhere from within sight of land to 100 miles out on Georges Bank. While the days are over when draggers came into Boston and New Bedford with hundreds of thousands of pounds of flounder, perhaps our fisheries will see those days return. Meanwhile, many smallboat fishermen throughout the Cape & Islands are still able to bring in flounder each day to meet local needs. Even our longline fishermen hook some gorgeous black-backs among the cod and pollock.

Just yesterday, I saw fifty pounds of *slammers* being unloaded. Some weighed four to five pounds each. In fact, as I write this, tomorrow is the first of May, opening day of the recreational season for flounder fishing. Many black-back flounder have wintered in the Cape's rivers, such as Bass River and Parkers River in Yarmouth, Mitchell River in Chatham, as well as estuaries throughout Nantucket and Martha's Vineyard. All will be loaded with eager fishermen and hungry flounder.

Swan River itself is frequently a hot spot for flounder fishing. We have seen some beauties brought out right here at our little bridge on Lower County Road; however, it is more common to see eels caught here. That's when the entertainment gets good, as amateur anglers stare in horror at a fat, eighteen-inch eel squirming around on their line. If they try to grab the thing, the eel just wraps around their wrists, and... Oh well, I don't want to lose any cooks here.

The finest eating fish of all the flounder is the grey sole. It varies in size from twelve to thirty inches. From my experience, flounder (in general) and grey sole (in particular) are the most difficult of all fish to fillet; even a large fish is only one or two inches thick. From this, you have to cut two fillets and remove the skin. As a result, roughly two-thirds of the fish goes into the barrel. So, if you start with a whole fish costing $1 to $3 per pound, you don't need a calculator to see where the cost comes from with these fish. The sweet, fresh fillets make them well worth the price.

Spring is also a great time to get clams of all kinds. As the winter winds and ice give way to sunshine and longer daylight hours, the steamers and quahogs (pronounced *koe-hogs*, please) rise up from their sandy depths. They are easier to dig, so suddenly all the hibernating shellfishermen appear with bushels of clean, meaty clams. And just as timely, folks start to think about their favorite shellfish.

Cape & Islands shellfishermen are a separate breed altogether. Self-proclaimed "River Rats," they are as independent and ornery as any cowboy who ever lived! I love them. They usually have very little in the way of material goods to show for their toil. They have little use for traditions of modern day. They love their independence, they could never deal with bosses or time-clocks, and they can hardly stand each other (related or not) as they team up in short-term alliances. But few people in any field of work put in as hard a day as our local shellfishermen.

And let me warn you: if a local shellfisherman challenges you to arm wrestle, graciously defer! All that mud-digging makes strong muscles.

Cape Cod, Nantucket & Martha's Vineyard benefit from being one of the most shellfish rich areas along the Atlantic seaboard. With the exception of Chesapeake Bay, we are one of the furthest points south for finding steamer (*softshell*) clams, and we are the furthest point north for native quahogs (*hardshell* clams). We also have in abundance sea (or *surf*) clams, to which we can add our fabulous oysters, scallops, blue mussels, and conchs to complete a shellfish lover's heaven.

One of the first methods of employment I sought out on Cape Cod was that of a shellfisherman. (I would have to get humorist Dave Barry to write that book, funnier than fiction.) But I learned a lot. I firmly believe that you have to be born to that sort of work. Oh, I did make some money at it. No denying that. In fact, we often say that we built the house we live in with Cape scallops! Back in the 70s there was some great money to be made harvesting scallops. Even for a greenhorn, wash-ashore. I loved it, and it was hard for me to believe that it was a job.

Few people in any field of work put in as hard a day as do our local shellfishermen.

We would set out at sunrise in a twenty-foot boat, always in the fall, and we would drag along river and bay bottom in one of the prettiest places upon this earth. We would haul-up our small dredges, then cull out the money catch (bay scallops) from dinner (flounders, monkfish, clams, and whatever). And we always kept a five-gallon bucket full of seawater, into which went all the specimens for our 55-gallon aquarium back home.

Sure, it was work. Our backaches attested to that each night. But how could you measure the benefits of coming home with all those treats, a sun-burned and salty smile, *plus* a pocket full of cash, as well? Maybe someday I'll retire healthy and get back to a little shellfishing as a pastime.

So much for Scallop Dreams. Clams are a little different.

Quahogs are at their greatest abundance in the spring. The winter causes them to burrow deeply, and the clam flats often are inaccessible because of ice and rough waters. I know firsthand that trying to make a living digging clams in winter is difficult. More than one lean January I waded waist-deep into 35-degree water with a stiff wind piercing unseen openings in my gear and tried to put bread on the table with clam profits. If clams were priced as precious metals I would have been all set. I will have to say that it was character-building and leave it at that.

In the spring, clams rise close to the surface of their muddy homes. Springtime, and the diggin' is easy! Who wouldn't mind going out in that clear, warming air, soaking up the sights and sounds along the shore, playing in the mud, then going home with a decent day's pay?

A quahog is sold in three different sizes. The smallest legal size quahog is a *littleneck* clam. Measuring a minimum of an inch in thickness, littlenecks are either eaten raw on the half shell, or used whole in the shell for various soups and stews. The next grading for a quahog is a middle size called a *cherrystone*, measuring 2½ to 3 inches in diameter. Cherrystones are also popular eaten raw. As a quahog gets older and larger, it becomes a *chowder* clam. Measuring above 3½ inches, these clams are too big to be enjoyed raw, so they are generally shucked and used in various recipes calling for chopped clams. The quahog has a much more intense flavor than the other clams we have mentioned, but a truly good clam chowder really must have some quahog in it.

Seafood appeals to us,
in part,
because most of it
is still
a natural product.

The sea clam is a large softshell clam found in somewhat deeper waters. It has a much different flavor, sweeter and milder than a quahog, and they are often cut for so-called clam *strips* without the bellies (as opposed to *whole* fried clams). Though they are delicious, a chowder made only from sea clams would be like making spaghetti out of a can of *Franco-American*.

Sea clams are generally brought in by sixty-foot boats working close to shore. A day's catch might be two hundred bushels. Then comes the delightful job of shucking them. We used to shuck them in our market. Now, however, the Commonwealth requires elaborate shucking premises, and we lack the space. So we get ours shucked in Chatham.

The number of products made from sea clams is impressive. They are used in chowders, clam pies, frying strips, "clam tenders," clam fritters, and many other uses. And even the shells are put to good use. Throughout the Cape & Islands, they are not only found inside cottages as ashtrays, but also outside cottages to line walkways and driveways with their quaint white appearance. Aside from looking nice, they also let rainwater leach through, thus providing a far more ecologically sound surface than pavement. A classic example of early Yankee recycling!

One of the tastiest spring arrivals is the crab, which could almost be considered an underutilized species from local waters. The Cape & Islands have two types of edible crabs: blue crabs and rock crabs. Blue crabs are not fished commercially in our waters, and the only commercial operation I know is in another part of southeastern Massachusetts. While blue crabs are the pride of the Chesapeake area, they are still quite plentiful in our rivers and bays. In fact, crabbing is a popular pastime, and often you see families making a day of trying to catch the pesky critters.

Rock crabs, on the other hand, are caught commercially, and bear close resemblance in taste and appearance to the legendary stone crabs of Florida. Rock crabs are intertidal, meaning they are found in deeper saltwater, as opposed to the blue crabs found in the shallower, brackish waters of the estuaries. Rock crabs are considered a by-catch of lobstering, and often the lobstermen just throw them back.

For one thing, rock crabs are difficult to handle without having the crab handle you. And then once they have been landed and cooked, the battle is only half over. After all they are not called *rock* crabs, because they play guitars! Shucking them requires a mallet or heavy knife, and a *lot* of patience. All that said, however, the result is well worth it. Many people prefer the sweet meat from these crabs over lobster meat.

I think that one of the saddest developments in the world of food technology must certainly be that mock crabmeat sold in supermarkets as *seafood salad*, also known as *surimi*. It's a crabmeat product, which contains mostly fish, lots of sugar, red food dye, and 15% crabmeat and crab *shells*. This ubiquitous product is being served all over the country in the guise of crabmeat, crab stuffing, and other crab recipes.

That's really a shame, not only because quality is being sacrificed for profit, but also because the public's taste for the real thing is being altered. So, when people say that food doesn't taste as good as it did in the old days, I couldn't agree more. So much of our food today is altered. Seafood appeals to us in part, because most of it is still a natural product, the same today as it was centuries ago...*if* you are buying it prudently.

Spring on the Cape & Islands clearly brings an abundance of seafood to the tables. My old friend, fishing partner, and fellow fishmonger, George Vining of George's Fish Market in Harwichport often would say: "There's no reason for any able-bodied person to either go hungry or wanting for work on Cape Cod. The shores around us are full of opportunity."

Opportunity not to get rich necessarily, but certainly to eat as a King!

Gourmet Pizza with White Clam Sauce

Bob and I thank our chef, Glen Woodworth, for this clever variation on the pizza theme, which can be served as an hors d'oeuvre for a crowd, or a filling lunch for four to six people.

Pizza dough is not really difficult to make. Before you roll out the pizza dough, though, consider how you will use the recipe. You may wish to make one big, rectangular crust, or else round individual pizzas.

This sauce can be made using all quahogs or a combination of half quahogs/half sea clams, which is what we prefer. The quahogs have a full, salty flavor, while the sea clams are somewhat sweeter and more bland. Whatever you decide, if the clams are not available in half-pints, you could make a double batch and freeze whatever you don't use.

For the pizza dough:

1 cup lukewarm water	¼ teaspoon black pepper
1 teaspoon sugar	¼ teaspoon salt
1 packet of yeast	½ teaspoon each: onion powder,
2 tablespoons olive oil	garlic powder, crushed red pepper,
3½ cups flour	and oregano

For the clam sauce:

4 tablespoons olive oil	1 pint clam juice
3 cloves of garlic, chopped	1 teaspoon oregano
1 cup chopped onion	1 teaspoon basil
½ pint chopped quahogs	1 tablespoon fresh parsley, chopped
½ pint chopped sea clams	Fresh ground black pepper

For the topping:

Grated mozzarella cheese	Dried oregano
Sliced fresh tomatoes	

Stir the sugar into the warm water then add the yeast and mix until it is dissolved. Let it sit for five minutes to activate.

Combine the dry ingredients in a large mixing bowl. Add the oil to the yeast mixture, then pour it into the flour mix, stirring until all the flour is incorporated. Turn the dough onto a lightly-floured surface and knead it for five minutes. Return the dough to the mixing bowl, cover it with a clean, damp cloth, and set it in a warm, draft-free place to rise for one hour or until it is about double its original size.

Note: Your oven can be the perfect place to raise dough. Turn the oven to 200 degrees for a minute, then turn it off. Open the door for a few minutes to cool it down, then place the dough inside and close the door. Just remember not to turn on the heat while the dough is in it!

Using a rubber spatula, turn the dough out onto a lightly-floured board or countertop. Knead it briefly, then divide it into four equal segments, forming each into a ball. Cover them with a damp towel and allow them to rest for ten minutes before rolling them out.

Preheat the oven to 400 degrees.

Using a lightly-floured rolling pin, roll out each dough ball to a quarter-inch thickness then place on a sheet pan to bake. Bake for ten to fifteen minutes or until the top is golden brown in places and puffed-up well. Set the crust aside until you are ready to use.

In a large skillet, heat the oil. Add the garlic and onion, then cook on medium heat until the onions are clear. Add the clams and cook for five minutes, stirring occasionally. Pour in the clam juice and herbs, then bring to a gentle boil. If you won't be using the sauce right away, turn off the heat to prevent overcooking the clams and making them tough.

Using a slotted spoon, ladle clam sauce onto the cooked pizza shell. Cover with a light layer of cheese, then top each pizza with several tomato slices and a sprinkling of oregano. Bake on a sheet pan for ten to fifteen minutes until the cheese begins to brown and bubble.

Remove the pizza to a cutting board, cut into slices and serve.

Spring Appetizer

Quahog

Dairy-Free Clam Chowder

Serves 4 to 6

This recipe was developed for a friend who was allergic to milk, but still very fond of clams. It is delicious as presented here; however, you could easily add milk or cream at the end to please any traditionalists.

4 tablespoons vegetable oil	5 medium potatoes
4 tablespoons flour	1 cup of clam broth
2 onions, diced	1 cup of water
1 pint of chopped quahogs, sea clams, or both	¼ teaspoon white pepper

Peel and dice the potatoes. In a small saucepan, boil them with two cups of water until they are soft. Allow them to cool slightly, then remove about a third of the potatoes and all of the cooking liquid to a blender. Process them until it is a smooth purée. Set this and the remaining cooked potatoes aside.

In a four-quart saucepan, heat the oil, add in the onions, and cook on medium heat until they are clear. Add the flour and cook, stirring constantly, for five minutes.

Slowly pour in the broth and water, stirring with a wire whisk to eliminate the lumps. Sprinkle the white pepper over the mixture and allow it to come to the boiling point.

Carefully add the clams, stir them in, reduce the heat to low and simmer for ten to fifteen minutes, stirring occasionally. The clams should firm-up, but still be tender. Remember, overcooking will make them tough.

The potatoes and their purée may be added now. Allow the chowder to heat thoroughly.

Ladle into bowls, then garnish with chopped parsley, scallions, or both.

Sole Oscar

Serves 4

Timing is important, so I recommend that you assemble all of the ingredients and necessary appliances, then plan to make the Hollandaise while the fish and asparagus are cooking. Though the sauce should be kept warm, it does contain uncooked eggs and must not be held for long.

For those who may wish to do without Hollandaise, this can still be a wonderfully satisfying, as well as a low cholesterol meal, if served with a juicy lemon wedge on the side.

    4 medium to large sole fillets
    4 ounces of crabmeat
    12 stalks of asparagus

For a fool-proof Hollandaise sauce:

    2 egg yolks   Pinch of white pepper
    ¼ teaspoon salt   2 tablespoons lemon juice
    ¾ cup of drawn* butter

To prepare the fish and asparagus:

Preheat the oven to 400 degrees. Arrange a single layer of sole in a shallow baking dish. Spread the crabmeat over the fillets, add a few tablespoons of water to the pan, then cover it with foil wrap. If you have used a metal pan, the fish will cook in about ten minutes. A glass or ceramic dish takes longer to heat up, so your dinner may take twenty minutes. In either case, sole is a delicate item and should not be overcooked. Take a peek under the foil to check for doneness. The fish will flake easily and be opaque throughout when it is finished.

As the fish bakes, steam the asparagus in a frying pan until it's tender.

To prepare the sauce:

Put the egg, lemon juice, salt and pepper into a blender and process briefly. While the blade is running, slowly drizzle in the butter. Continue to blend for a moment longer and *Voilà!* You've made Hollandaise.

To present each serving:

Carefully lift the fish onto individual plates. Lay three pieces of asparagus on top, then ladle a generous serving of sauce across it.

*The clear, yellow liquid which has risen above the milky sediment.

This culinary classic transposes beautifully to the seafood realm!

Flounder Florentine with Cream Sauce

Serves 4 to 6

2 pounds of fillets provides six small or four medium portions

For the spinach mix:
One 10-ounce package of frozen chopped spinach
or one package of fresh spinach
2 tablespoons butter or margarine
¼ cup onion, diced fine   Pinch of nutmeg
½ cup bread crumbs   Splash of Pernod (optional)
¼ cup Parmesan cheese   Salt and pepper to taste

For the cream sauce:
4 tablespoons butter or margarine 1 cup milk or cream
4 tablespoons flour   Dash of Tabasco sauce
1 cup fish stock (See *KitchenNotes*.) Dash of Worcestershire sauce
                                   Salt to taste

Melt the butter in a small sauté pan and add the onions. Cook on medium heat until the onions are clear. Clean the spinach. Frozen spinach must be defrosted and squeezed dry; fresh spinach must have stems and tough leaves removed, then be steamed before chopping. Place all the remaining ingredients in a bowl and mix together with the cooked onions and butter. Set aside until ready for assembly.

In a small saucepan, melt the butter. Add the flour and cook together on medium heat, stirring constantly for about 5 minutes. Add the Tabasco and Worcestershire to the fish stock, then pour the fish stock slowly into the flour mix, stirring all the while with a wire whisk to eliminate lumps. Add the cream in the same manner, then reduce the heat and let the sauce cook for five to ten minutes, stirring frequently until it thickens.

Preheat the oven to 400 degrees.

There are a variety of ways to prepare the dish from this point. You may wish to place some stuffing on the fillet and roll it for baking, or you may prefer to lay a fillet in the pan, spread some spinach mix upon it, then top it with another piece of fish. I have also used this stuffing with larger fillets, such as scrod, haddock or whiting. In that case, I create a pocket by making a diagonal cut down from the top of the fillet, then stuff the pocket with the spinach mix.

In any case, place your fish in a shallow baking pan, cover it with foil and bake it for ten minutes. Remove the fish from the oven, ladle the warm sauce over it, sprinkle with a little Parmesan cheese, then return it uncovered to the oven for five to ten minutes. The time in the oven depends upon the thickness of the fish and the temperature of your own oven, so be certain to check for doneness. (See *Kitchen Notes*.)

Mackerel en Papillote

For each person allow:
    1 large or 2 small fillets
    Thinly-sliced onion
    1 tablespoon of sherry
    Salt and pepper
    Parchment paper or aluminum foil

Preheat the oven to 400 degrees.

For each serving, fold a piece of parchment paper in half and cut an elongated semi-circle two or three inches larger than the individual fillets. Open out the folded paper and place a serving of fish upon on it, near the fold. Top with a thin onion slice, sprinkle the onion with a tablespoon of sherry, then season with salt and pepper. Fold down the other half of the parchment and crimp together the top and bottom edges to make a packet.

Place the packets on a baking sheet and cook for ten to fifteen minutes, depending upon the size of the fillets.

Packets may be placed on individual plates and opened with a knife at the table. The aroma of the escaping steam is part of the enjoyment of a fish cooked in parchment. (You may wish to tell your guests that they don't need to eat the paper.)

Salmon in Filo with Scallion Remoulade

This is elegant fare for entertaining or jazzing up a family dinner. Filo dough is readily available in the freezer of most grocery stores. For best results, allow it to defrost for twenty-four hours in your refrigerator. While it does have a reputation for being temperamental, filo can be managed quite well with a little practice and patience. I am always grateful that there are so many sheets in one box; if one or two of them tear or dry out, there are still plenty left. The results are always spectacular and worth the effort!

Fish in filo can be prepared up to a day before it is baked. Place the wrapped pieces on a baking sheet in the refrigerator. Cover loosely. Cook according to directions when needed.

For each person, allow:
    6 to 8 ounces of skinless salmon fillet
    Scallion greens, cut into ¼-inch lengths
    Melted butter or margarine

For 1¼ cups of scallion remoulade:

2 egg yolks	Pinch white pepper
2 tablespoons lemon juice	1 tablespoon parsley, chopped
1 teaspoon grated lemon rind	¼ cup chopped scallions
Dash of salt	1 cup salad oil

Put all the ingredients for the remoulade, except for the oil, into a blender and process briefly to mince the herbs. In a slow, steady stream, pour the oil into the blender while it is running. When all the oil has been added, stop the blades to scrape down the sides of the container. Process for another thirty seconds to be sure the sauce is thoroughly blended, then refrigerate.

To prepare the filo packets:
Carefully unfold the filo dough onto a clean work space. Keep a clean, dampened kitchen towel handy to lay over the unused sheets in case you are interrupted, or they begin to dry while you are working.

Peel off a sheet of the dough, lay it on the counter and brush it with melted butter. Lay another sheet of dough on top of the first, brush it with melted better, and repeat the procedure. Cut the three layers in half widthwise.

Place a piece of fish (skin-side down) on the filo about two inches in from the long side of the rectangle. Sprinkle a few scallions on the fillet, then begin to wrap by lifting the two-inch edge of filo up to the fish and rolling the dough and fish over once. Pick up the flaps of dough on either side and fold them onto what is now the top. Continue to roll the fish and filo, keeping the edges tucked in, until you have run out of dough.

Place the packet onto a buttered cookie pan, and make sure that the edge of dough is tucked under the fish. Ideally, the scallions will have ended up on top of the fish. If not, adjust the original placement of the next fillet onto the filo. Lightly brush the top of each packet with butter.

Bake in a preheated 375-degree oven for twenty to twenty-five minutes until the dough is well-browned.

Serve with a generous dollop of scallion remoulade on the side.

Mackerel with Sesame-Dijon Glaze

A snap to prepare, this recipe gives mackerel a tasty lift!

Allow 6 to 8 ounces of fish per person

Blending together equal parts mayonnaise and Dijon mustard, mix up as much glaze as you will need. Place the fish in a shallow baking dish for broiling. Spread the glaze on the fish, then sprinkle with sesame seeds.

Place under the broiler (not too close to the heat) and cook for five to ten minutes. Check often to see that the top is not cooking too quickly. If it is, move it further from the heat and continue cooking until the flesh flakes easily with a fork.

Spring Entrée

Atlantic Salmon

Smoked Salmon Primavera

Serves 4

1 package fresh fettucine (or 8 ounces dry)
2 cups thinly-julienned broccoli, carrots, zucchini, summer squash, red or green peppers, or mushrooms (choose 4 or 5)

4 tablespoons olive oil	1 tablespoon parsley, chopped
3 cloves of garlic, diced fine	2 scallions, cut into ¼-inch pieces
1 small onion, in thin wedges	12 black olives, sliced in thirds
2 cups light cream	½ cup Parmesan cheese
Fresh ground black pepper	8 ounces smoked salmon
1 teaspoon basil	

Prepare the fettucine according to package directions, but undercook it slightly. Set it aside.

In a ten-inch skillet, heat two tablespoons of the oil. Add the garlic and onions, then sauté on medium heat until the onions are clear. Add in the rest of the oil, as well as your selection of julienned vegetables, tossing the pan a few times so they will be coated with the oil. Pour in a quarter cup of water, cover and cook on medium heat for five minutes. To retain their color and just a little crispness, the vegetables should be lightly cooked.

Add in the cooked fettucine, cream, cheese, pepper and basil. When this mixture is heated through, add in all of the remaining ingredients, except for a few olive slices and some parsley for garnish.

Gently stir the mixture to prevent breaking up the fish pieces and continue cooking on medium to low heat until it is hot throughout.

Turn the primavera onto a warmed platter or individual plates, garnish with olives and parsley, then serve.

Squid Bolognase

With garlic toast rounds, this may be used as an appetizer for 6; over pasta, this recipe can serve as an entrée for 4.

For either use:

1 pound squid (See *Kitchen Notes*.)	½ teaspoon oregano
1 clove of garlic, minced	½ teaspoon thyme
1 medium onion, diced	½ teaspoon basil
2 tablespoons olive oil	½ tablespoon parsley, chopped
1 28-ounce can plum tomatoes,	½ teaspoon salt
well-drained and chopped	Fresh ground pepper to taste

Clean the squid and slice into rings, but keep the tentacles whole.

Put the oil into a heated sauté pan, add the garlic and onions, then cook until they are clear. Add the tomatoes and seasonings, then gently simmer for ten minutes. Drain the squid of excess water and add it to the simmering tomato mixture. Maintain medium heat. Stir periodically as the temperature rises. Once the mixture resumes a gentle boil, set the timer for five minutes. Stir occasionally to ensure even cooking.

Serve immediately to prevent overcooking.

For garlic toast rounds:

1 loaf French bread about 2 or 3 inches in diameter
1 clove garlic, minced
½ cup melted margarine or oil
1 teaspoon parsley, chopped

Cut the bread into one-inch slices and toast both sides lightly under the broiler. Mix together the melted butter, garlic, and parsley, then spread onto toast rounds and heat until the butter bubbles.

Shrimp & Clams with Linguine

Serves 2

1 dozen littleneck clams, rinsed well
1 dozen medium shrimp, uncooked, peeled, and deveined
1 large tomato, sliced into thin wedges
2 scallions, cut into ¼-inch lengths
1 clove of garlic, diced fine
2 tablespoons olive oil
¼ cup white wine
6 ounces of fresh linguine

Bring two quarts of water to a boil in a medium saucepan, then keep this hot while you prepare the clams and shrimp.

Rinse the clams well. Peel and devein the shrimp. (See *Kitchen Notes*.)

Pour the olive oil into a heated ten-inch skillet, add the garlic, and cook on medium heat for two or three minutes. Add in the whole clams with one cup of water, cover the pan, and turn the heat on high.

Cook the linguine according to package directions, which usually takes three to five minutes in boiling water. Make sure the strands are separated well as you put them into the water.

Check the clams after they have been cooking for five minutes. They should have popped open in that time. If not, cover the pan and cook for another minute or two. Add the shrimp, tomatoes, scallions, and wine to the boiling broth. Cover and cook for two minutes, shaking the pan once or twice to ensure even cooking.

Test the linguine. If it is done, drain the water and hold the pasta hot until the shrimp and clams are ready. You may want to toss it with a little olive oil to keep it from sticking.

Divide the pasta into two portions on soup plates or in shallow bowls. Spoon the clams and shrimp onto each serving, then pour the broth over it all. Serve with Parmesan cheese.

Note: Fresh linguine cooks in less time than dry pasta. So, if you use dry pasta, begin cooking it as soon as this pasta water boils, before starting to cook the clams.

Shad Roe

Serves 2

We thank Dot Hoskins for her input on the preparation of this seasonal delicacy. As with all seafood, the key is not to overcook it!

4 pieces of bacon
2 sets of shad roe

In a medium skillet, cook the four pieces of bacon until crisp. Remove the bacon from the pan and allow the fat to cool only slightly before laying two sets of roe in the pan. Turn the sets over at once so they are coated with the bacon drippings. Cover the pan and cook on medium to low heat for ten to fifteen minutes, turning once.

Serve with the bacon and hot, parsleyed potatoes for a meal that has satisfied generations of shore dwellers!

For seafood lovers, spring has not arrived until the first shad roe has appeared.

Linguine with White Clam Sauce

Serves 4 to 6

As mentioned in preparing the Gourmet Pizza (page 20), this recipe can be made using all quahogs or a combination of half quahogs/half sea clams.

4 tablespoons olive oil	1 pint clam juice
3 cloves of garlic, chopped fine	1 tablespoon fresh parsley, chopped
1 cup chopped onion	1 teaspoon basil
½ pint chopped quahogs	1 teaspoon oregano
½ pint chopped sea clams	Fresh ground black pepper to taste

In a large skillet, heat the oil. Add the garlic and onion, then cook on medium until the onions are clear. Add the clams and cook for five minutes, stirring occasionally. Add the juice and herbs, then bring to a gentle boil.

If you won't be using the sauce right away, turn off the heat to prevent overcooking the clams and making them tough.

Following the directions on the package, cook the linguine until it is *al dente*. Add this to the sauce and simmer together for one or two minutes, allowing the pasta to absorb some of the liquid and a lot of the flavor. You may add a little extra water at this time to make more sauce.

Adjust the seasonings and serve immediately. Don't forget the Parmesan or Romano cheese!

Scrod San Sebastian

Scrod San Sebastian is a perennial favorite at our restaurant. The dish was inspired by a meal we enjoyed in the town of the same name on the northern coast of Spain. There the original recipe was made with a steaked white fish, but we have adapted it for the American palate which prefers to see the fish on the plate *without* its skin and bones.

For each person, allow:
    2 teaspoons butter or margarine
    ¼ teaspoon chopped garlic
    6 to 8 ounces fresh scrod or other white fish
    3 or 4 littleneck clams, rinsed well
    ¼ cup water
    2 teaspoons scallions, chopped
    1 teaspoon parsley, chopped

Because the fish fillets are somewhat delicate, it is best not to prepare a large quantity in one pan. A serving for four should be the maximum in a ten-inch pan. If you are making five to eight servings, use two frying pans at once and arrange the seafood so it is only one layer deep. By the same token, if you are making only one or two servings, use a small enough pan so that the fish simmers in the juices.

Begin by heating a frying pan of appropriate size, adding the oil, then the garlic and cooking briefly. Add the remaining ingredients in the order listed, making certain to snuggle the clams in around the fish pieces. Cover and cook on medium heat until the clams are all open (Depending on the quantities involved, this should be about ten to fifteen minutes.)

Taking care that the fish pieces don't fall apart, use a spoon or spatula to transfer the fish and the clams either to a serving dish, or to individual dishes. Pour the liquid over the rest and serve.

Spring Entrée

*This makes
a delightful meal
when served with
a crisp green salad
and
a loaf of crusty bread
to dip in the broth.*

Appetizers
Mussels Diablo
Crabmeat Cocktail with Dijon Sauce
Crabmeat Spread on Toast Rounds
Marinated Mussels

Soup
Key West Conch Chowder

Salads
Seafood Pasta Salad
Calamari Salad

Entrées
Chilled Poached Halibut with Dijon Sauce
Oriental Steamed Salmon
Blackened Salmon
Striped Bass in Filo with Red Pepper Mayonnaise
Grilled Swordfish
Seafood en Brochette
Grilled Yellowfin Tuna with Tomato Mint Sauce
Grilled Fresh Tuna with Rosemary Lime Marinade
Grilled Striped Bass with Fresh Fruit Salsa
Mako Shark Steak au Poivre

SUMMER

C. Ahern

The Summer Catch

Originally only a seasonal market catering to the summer trade, Swan River Fish Market was born in summertime, when the population increases ten times that of the locals throughout Cape Cod, Nantucket & Martha's Vineyard. Then it took some forty years to work up the nerve to remain open on a year-round basis.

Coincidentally, the fresh seafood selection increases tremendously during summer as well. Striped bass, bluefish, tuna, swordfish, lobsters (inshore), shark, and eels are among the many delights that begin to surface in our market during those weeks, and we decide upon the "catch of the day" for our restaurant only after seeing what the fishermen arrive with off the boat that morning. Truly, the meal is *the* catch of the day.

Clearly, then, summer is a season of plenty: of fresh fish, of people, and of work! But it gets our juices running, and it's really plenty of fun.

The first bluefish we see of the season are taken out of the weir traps in Nantucket Sound. By then, sport fishermen who really know their stuff have already been catching them for a month. The early hot spots are on the south sides of the islands of Nantucket and Martha's Vineyard, as well as off Popponesset Beach in Mashpee. These first bluefish to arrive are called *racers*. Generally full-grown, adult fish, they are thin and scrawny from their long journey.

Truly a gamefish, blues often are caught by anglers who just love to catch fish, not eat them. Left in the sun for any time at all and improperly handled, their catch is easily ruined. So, we turn away such fish all summer. In fact, those weekend Yahoos in their boat-toys who literally destroy schools of bluefish are the bane of real fishermen.

Bluefish aside, striped bass are *the* premier gamefish to inhabit Cape & Islands waters. Stripers are regarded as highly for their difficulty to catch, as they are for their fine taste. Now added to the striped bass' eminent stature is their legendary comeback.

Five years ago, the species was on the verge of extinction. Like many of our fish resources, they were overfished, polluted out of their spawning grounds, and nearly wiped out of their ocean habitat altogether. But through fishing conservation laws put into effect along the eastern seaboard, bass have made a terrific rebound. Generally, there are so few bright spots for wild fish lovers to look at with so many fish resources at all-time lows; however, striped bass have proven that with proper efforts, the oceans can be managed and harvested to feed a hungry world.

In 1994, Massachusetts law allows only a set quota of stripers to be caught beginning on the first of July. All fishermen must have permits, and a striped bass must measure a full thirty-six inches in length to be a *keeper*. Any striper measuring less must be released alive. This has been the law since 1991, and the summer of 1993 brought more striped bass to these waters than any of our fishermen could recall ever seeing. Long after the commercial season for catching striped bass had ended, tremendous numbers of stripers were still sighted basking in warm waters around Cape Cod, Nantucket & Martha's Vineyard.

Yet another interesting summer arrival to Cape & Islands waters is shark, which were ignored by most fishermen for many years. I first saw people eating them when I was attempting to support the family as a commercial fisherman in the Florida Keys. Until then, I had thought it was only the other way around: shark eats man.

In Florida, sharks were a constant problem when I was fishing for king mackerel. All too often I would pull in my catch, only to see a blue or a hammerhead shark take it from me at the side of the boat. Once they had found our fishing spot, we would have to move on, leaving behind our huge school of mackerel. Any time we caught a black-tip or a lemon shark, though, that fish was destined for the grill.

In our northern waters, mako is the best shark for flavor. Cecy and I first featured mako on our Swan River menu at least ten years ago, when it was a novelty, and people were full of both questions and doubt. That's no longer the case, however, and now even mako are overfished and regulated. So, we list it on the menu as *when available*. Sharks are one of the slowest growing fish in the sea, so their increasing popularity has led to their scarcity. Perhaps new fishing regulations will allow mako to rebound as stripers did.

Dreaded by our cod fishermen, sand sharks (also known as dogfish, Cape dogfish, etc.) are also extremely abundant in summer. When the dogs show up, many a cod fisherman has been known to haul in his gear

Striped bass

and head for shore. Historically, dogfish has had little or no commercial value, and their numbers make other fish difficult to catch.

In the past two years, however, dogfish has become a targeted species around our waters. With cod, haddock, and flounder so hard to find, the market for dogfish has opened up considerably. Still, 90% of the catch is shipped out of the country, where much of it ends up being served as fish & chips in England. While it is an excellent tasting fish, dogfish remains very difficult to process. Unfortunately, we are not able to take advantage of this resource, and we just watch it get boxed up and trucked off-Cape.

One of the grandest fish in the sea must be halibut, which are caught in cold water oceans throughout many parts of the world. And while halibut used to be very plentiful on Georges Bank, some seventy-five miles east of Nantucket, catching a local halibut now is like finding gold.

I can remember unloading halibut by the dozens at the Chatham fish pier twenty years ago, where each year a fishbuyer from New York's Fulton Market would offer a $100 bonus to the Chatham fisherman who caught the largest halibut during the month of May. So, that wise old fishmonger ended up with some of the largest, freshest halibut along the eastern seaboard. Unfortunately, no undersize limit then existed for halibut. Today, a solitary halibut landing turns many a head on the dock.

Tuna are yet another of our most spectacular summer visitors. In years past, the only people we knew who ate fresh tuna were either adventurous fishermen, or else travelers from the Mediterranean or the Orient. In fact, when I first was introduced to fresh tuna, I was told it had to be soaked overnight in milk or marinade to make it palatable. Wow, what a waste! As we now know, fresh tuna, grilled quickly, then topped with a nice salsa or sauce can be as satisfying as any steak.

Carefully monitored and regulated now, tuna can be caught only by fishermen who have a special permit. The fish is individually tagged, and the buyer must log all catches for weekly reporting to the state and federal governments. When the annual quota is reached for each type (bluefin, big-eye, yellowfin, etc.), then fishing is closed until the next year. Nothing is harder for a captain to do in September than to head for the fishing grounds as tuna leap all around and know that the season is closed. He can look, but he cannot touch. And when one tuna might be worth $15,000 on the Japanese market, it's better for him not to look!

Rod-and-reel tuna fishing is one of the nicest jobs I've ever observed. Oh yes, it's risky and often unproductive. And it involves an initial investment of tens of thousands of dollars, as well as a ton of experience. I had the great fortune to go with a commercial boat out of Harwichport with Captain Pat Hynes a couple of years back, and what a life! You steam out of port for an hour or two. You stop, set your trolls at your favorite spot, then sit back and wait. And watch.

The beauty of the day is only part of the job. Tuna are generally found in the same feeding areas as whales and dolphins. So, while you wait for the fussy tuna to consider striking your lure, you are treated to a show that whale-watching boats all pray for. While not a single tuna might ever strike your bait, dozens of whales and porpoises are likely to play all day. In fact, most boats have more empty-handed trips than productive ones, but what a *great* day at the office!

The fish that probably give me the greatest optimism are salmon. Twenty years ago they were almost unheard of, except in summer: salmon and peas on the 4th of July, one of the classic fish-holidays. I never realized this, however, until I worked in a fish market during that time of year. During June, we would be selling fifty pounds of salmon a week; then Mr. Folsom, my fish-mentor, would order three hundred or four hundred pounds for the first week of July! And we never seemed to have enough.

Back then, most salmon were flown in from Alaska and the Pacific Northwest, but we would acquire some higher-priced Atlantic salmon for our fussiest customers. Though Atlantic salmon range from the Gulf of Maine to Nova Scotia, the stock was so low that the fishery all but ended.

Today salmon have become the premier farmed, or *aquacultured* fish in the world. Norway was the first country to develop farm-raised production, Great Britain, Chile, and Canada all followed closely behind. So successful were their efforts that too many fish were brought to market and prices collapsed. Buying Salmon became a United Nations experience, and we have benefited from this development. Small salmon farms now are found close enough to us that we can simply call the farmer and order fish for the next day. They are of superior quality, as fresh as any fish our boats are bringing in.

Salmon aquaculture has proven that seafood has a future. Many other types of fish and shellfish are also being farmed-raised successfully, including local mussels, oysters and quahogs. Not only does this guarantee us high quality seafood, but also it reduces pressure on wild stocks, thus improving the future for our local fishermen.

While we're on the topic of local shellfish, this season seems to be a natural time to enjoy all kinds. So natural, in fact, that you wonder whether our shellfishermen should really get paid during summer.

Just look where they work: along the beach, on sandbars that pop-up at low tide, in meandering rivers on quiet mornings, where they are joined only by gulls, geese, terns, and blue herons. Their biggest occupational hazards are greenhead flies and sunburns. Then they come into the market with their cut-off shorts, four-wheel drives, and maybe a cold beer to quench their thirst. For *this* they get paid? Yes, they *demand* money for what they've just plucked from the wild! (Sorry, I couldn't resist a joke from one of my favorite fishcutters, Franny Coe. The last thing any fisherman wants to hear is that he "got it for nothing." And I know from experience how hard they do work for those clams.)

Shellfish are easier to harvest in the summertime, because all the different types of clams rise closer to the surface during warm weather. The seas are generally calmer as well. One hazard that increases in summer, however, is pollution. With greater numbers of people, boats, and seabirds comes greater numbers of pollutants. As in most states, clean water monitoring has increased tremendously in Massachusetts during the past twenty years. We are required to follow strict guidelines, known as the "Shellfish Traceability Program," which works to protect your health.

Any waterway which is open to commercial shellfishing must be tested constantly, and our fishermen must identify specifically where they obtained their shellfish. We must document this, including a tag which must travel with the shellfish to the fish market, the restaurant, or wherever it is destined. That tag must be kept for ninety days after the shellfish is consumed, so any problems can be easily traced to the source. If you buy shellfish from a dealer you know and trust, you are totally safe in eating shellfish, raw or cooked. Of course, this doesn't make good copy for the media, so don't expect to hear about it from them.

Shellfish are tricky to handle properly, and mishandling does occur out there. Storage, rotation, temperature, cleanliness all are very important. But if you purchase shellfish from a reputable dealer, the delight of fresh shellfish is not a thing of the past.

Steamers are one of the best and most abundant shellfish on the Cape & Islands. But what do you do about the sand? When I was a boy, my family always summered in Maine, where I remember the first time digging clams in some wonderful, soft, black mud, somewhere near Bar Harbor. What a joyous discovery! But there was no sand to worry about. No grit. No crunch. Not at all like steamers around Cape Cod, Nantucket & Martha's Vineyard. When I finally dug clams from these waters I realized why. The clams live in sand, not mud! Simple, huh?

So how do you get the sand out of our clams? I love to hear all the methods that people boast of knowing. Its almost like hiccup cures. They all sound great. Some work some of the time. The best one is to put pepper on them, and they will sneeze the sand out. I refuse to tell you that my method is the right one. I'll just tell you what we do.

*If you
purchase shellfish
from a reputable dealer,
the delight
of fresh shellfish
is not
a thing of the past.*

We are fortunate enough to have on premise a $10,000 sand-purging system which provides a constant flow of refrigerated, oxygenated saltwater that runs through ultraviolet light to kill any bacteria. The clams must be in this for several days to get out all the sand. If you leave clams in a bucket of saltwater, they suffocate. So, if you do try a home remedy, first get advice from someone who has tried it.

Cape Cod, Nantucket & Martha's Vineyard benefit from an abundant resource of quahogs, those hardshell clams known in the marketplace as *littlenecks*, *cherrystones*, and *chowder clams*. Though they are found all the way down to Florida, a coldwater quahog (meatier, saltier, and cleaner-tasting) far outshines any clam I've tasted from Southern waters.

Digging quahogs is one of the most satisfying times I've spent at the shore. While sunbathing on a beach never appealed to me, not everyone sees the virtues in "scratching" for clams. You have to go out in wader boots two hours before low tide to stand in water about three feet deep. And there you harvest nature's garden with a 4-pronged rake. Each time you strike a clam, you hear a *ping*. (A *pong* is only a rock!) You pull the quahog out of its muddy bed, measure it for legal size, then either keep it, or toss it back. Scratching the right spot for two hours on either side of low tide, a real quahogger can make a day's pay.

Bullraking is another method of quahogging. This is done from a boat at high tide. The bullrake is a thirty-foot aluminum extension rake, which requires the strength of a… (You guessed it!) Fortunately, both of these ancient forms of shellfishing are still in common practice on the Cape & Islands today. Although aquaculture is on the increase, most of the clams we sell are still a wild product.

Conch is most commonly associated with the Caribbean, so not many people realize that Nantucket Sound and many of the rivers and bays throughout this area are loaded with this shellfish. While Cecy's recipe for conch chowder is derived from many tastings in the Florida Keys, anyone eating the dish down there is eating conch meat from the Philippines or the Bahamas. In our waters, though, we are able to harvest conch throughout the year, where they are a bountiful food source. Still, conchs are considered a nuisance. They devour other shellfish, such as scallops and clams, and they are not a joy to clean, but

Mussels are yet another example of one person's trash being another's treasure. How could mussels have gone unnoticed throughout these parts for so long? Of course, we all knew they were there. For years, we would run aground on islands of them at low tide, and all the sea ducks and gulls would feast on them. And for years, there was little or no market for them. No longer. The word is out. And the mussels are running out fast.

Five years ago the legal limit for a day's catch of mussels in Chatham was two hundred bushels. Boat after boat would land with their limit. Now the mussel resource in Chatham is almost gone. Heavy fishing, shifting sands, and voracious birds all have contributed to their demise. Fortunately, several local fishermen have successful mussel farms working in areas like Pleasant Bay and Town Cove in Orleans, and various spots in Eastham and Provincetown. Mussels grow fast, and they multiply quickly. All they need is clean, cold water, and proper management.

Mussels are the shellfish of the people. Long appreciated by French chefs, you can buy a generous serving for $1. Whether they are on the menu at our house or not, I can't resist scooping a handful whenever I'm kayaking around Morris Island in Chatham. (Of course, I do have a Chatham shellfish license. Don't leave home without it.)

Lobsters are a large part of our world throughout the Cape & Islands. It's funny, but whenever I travel to Florida or the West Coast or even the Caribbean, North Atlantic Lobsters are referred to as *MAINE* lobsters. At least half of our first-time customers think that our lobsters must come from Maine; however, hundreds of thousands of pounds of lobsters are brought into port from the waters around the Cape & Islands. In fact, America's lobster fishery began here during the early Nineteenth Century, and the nation's first and only lobster hatchery remains on the Vineyard.

With ports from Sandwich to Provincetown, Cape Cod Bay is loaded with lobster pots all summer long, and scuba diving for lobsters in Cape Cod Bay is very popular. According to East Dennis resident, David Wallace, the best days to dive for lobsters out there are cloudy days. It seems that lobsters like to stroll the sandy bottom there when the sun isn't shining. And David tells me that on a good, cloudy day, he and his friends have caught up to thirty lobsters in a thirty-minute period. *How sweet it is!*

Most of the lobsters caught in Cape Cod Bay, though, are small, *chicken* lobsters that run up to 1½ pounds each. The Bay has a migratory lobster population, so few lobsters are found there in winter or spring, and most are caught from late spring through late fall.

While Nantucket Sound also has a large lobster population, the majority of our lobsters are caught east of Chatham: The Great Backside of the Cape. When I once asked one of our Chatham lobstermen how close his traps were to Nauset Beach, Sharkey grinned at me and replied, "Close enough to smell the suntan lotion." And he was serious.

The lobsters caught by our Chatham and Orleans boats are generally larger than those out of Cape Cod Bay. All lobsters molt or shed their shells, one or two times per year. When they are softshelled, they hibernate without eating. Consequently, when you open the shell you find very little meat. A one-pound hardshell lobster has four ounces of meat; however, the same size softshell lobster yields only two to three ounces of meat.

All summer long, when Maine is full of softshell *shedders*, our Chatham run is rock-hard. I'll never forget one of our lobstermen unloading his catch into our tank. One of the customers asked if our lobsters were hardshells. Bill just took out a nice three-pounder, put it on the concrete floor, then stood on the claw. All 240 pounds of him. The claw didn't give a bit, which told the customer all he wanted to know.

Lobstering would seem to be a fishery that is in decent shape. For years, there have been limits to the number of licenses in Massachusetts, there have been limits to the number of pots allowed per license, and data has been monitored to help manage this fishery. If such methods were applied to other fisheries twenty years ago, our cod and haddock stocks would not be in the sorry state that they are in now.

When our tanks are full, we know it's summertime. We have two separate lobster holding systems that can hold about two tons of lobsters altogether. While it is not unusual to see one lobsterman catch three hundred or four hundred pounds of lobster in one day, lobstering is extremely hard work, and it can be dangerous. But when the only traffic jam on the way to work is a few boats heading over the Chatham Bars, you've *got* to love it.

Cecy and I are not going to present any lobster recipes in this book. After all, why would you want to mess with such a natural flavor? Instead, we offer you these few simple directions. The best way to cook a lobster is to steam it with very little water. No salt. No beer. No seasonings. Just enough water to keep from boiling out. Bring the water to a full boil. Put in the larger lobsters first, then the smaller ones as the time requires. Place a lid on the pot. Wait for the second boil, then begin to time from that point. A good rule of thumb is to cook a one-pound lobster for fifteen minutes. For each pound over that allow five minutes.

The easiest way to tell if your lobster is cooked is to flip the tail out straight. If it snaps back quickly, give it a few more minutes. If it doesn't snap quickly it will be nice and tender. Unlike most foods, when a lobster is undercooked it is tough. The longer you cook it, the more tender it will become.

Lobster

Mussels Diablo

Serves 4 to 6

Spicy hot, but served chilled, this dish can be prepared ahead and presented as either a first course, or a luncheon salad on a bed of lettuce!

4 pounds of mussels in the shell (See *Kitchen Notes.*)

For the marinade:

1 cup white wine	2 tablespoons pimentos, sliced
½ cup vinegar	1 lemon, sliced thin
1½ cup oil	1 clove of garlic, chopped fine
4 jalapeño peppers, sliced thin*	1 teaspoon red pepper flakes
1 small Bermuda onion, thin wedges	

Clean the mussels well and remove the beards. In a large pot with one cup of water, steam the mussels for about ten minutes or until all the shells are open. Drain off the broth, which can be frozen for future use in seafood soups or sauces.

Arrange a single layer of mussels in a shallow pan and refrigerate them while you prepare the marinade.

Mix together all the marinade ingredients except the oil. Then add the oil, pouring in a slow steady stream, whisking continuously until it is blended well.

Once the mussels are chilled, put them into a glass dish and pour the marinade over them, stirring to be sure they are coated. Refrigerate for at least two hours, stirring occasionally.

* Be sure to wash your hands well after handling the peppers, because their oils are very strong and can burn sensitive tissues.

Crabmeat Cocktail with Dijon Sauce

We love crabmeat when it is *ultra* fresh, just out of the shell, well-chilled, and served with a Dijon sauce for dipping. Simply delicious!

Allow 4 ounces of fresh crabmeat per person

For the sauce:
Equal parts Dijon mustard and mayonnaise, using two tablespoons of each per person

Using a small plate for each person, arrange the crabmeat on a red lettuce leaf, set a generous dollop of sauce alongside the meat and garnish each with a thin lemon wedge.

Crabmeat Spread on Toast Rounds

Serves 6 to 8

1 loaf of French bread (about 2 or 3 inches in diameter is best)	
8 ounces of fresh crabmeat	½ teaspoon mustard powder
1 cup mayonnaise	¼ teaspoon garlic powder
2 tablespoons scallions, chopped	2 drops of Tabasco
½ cup Parmesan cheese	1½ teaspoons Worcestershire sauce

Cut the French bread into one-inch slices and lightly toast both sides under the broiler. Set aside.

Blend the mustard powder and garlic powder into the Parmesan cheese. Mix together the mayonnaise, cheese mixture, Worcestershire sauce and Tabasco. Taking care not to break up all the chunks, gently fold in the drained crabmeat.

Just before serving, spread the crabmeat mix on the toast rounds. Sprinkle with Parmesan cheese and heat under the broiler until lightly browned. Serve at once.

Rock crab

Marinated Mussels

Serves 4 to 6

4 pounds of mussels (See *Kitchen Notes*.)

For the marinade:

1 small Bermuda onion, cut into thin wedges

¼ cup white wine 1 tablespoon sugar
¼ cup red wine vinegar 1 teaspoon salt
¼ teaspoon thyme Pinch of white pepper
¼ teaspoon basil 1½ cups oil
¼ teaspoon oregano 2 cloves garlic, minced

In a large pot with one cup of water, steam mussels for about ten minutes, or until all the shells are open. Cool them and remove the meats from the shells. Refrigerate until needed.

Mix together all the marinade ingredients without the oil. Add the oil in a slow, steady stream, whisking to blend it well.

In a glass bowl, combine the mussels and marinade, stirring to coat all the meats. Chill for at least two hours, stirring periodically to ensure that the mussels will be evenly marinated.

Key West Conch Chowder

Serves 6 to 8

2 tablespoons olive oil	2 tablespoons sherry
2 cloves of garlic, diced fine	½ teaspoon Tabasco
1 large onion, diced	1 teaspoon thyme
½ green pepper, diced	1 tablespoon parsley, chopped
1 stalk of celery, diced	¼ teaspoon red pepper flakes
2 cups water	2 tablespoons lime juice
2 cups clam broth	1 tablespoon tomato paste
1 pound ground conch meat	Pinch of white pepper
1 cup crushed tomatoes	
2 potatoes: peeled, diced and cooked *al dente*	

Heat the olive oil in a large saucepan, then add the garlic, onion, green pepper, and celery. When the onions are clear, add the remaining ingredients and bring to the boiling point. Simmer for an hour.

If the chowder becomes too thick, you may wish to add more water.

Why travel to Florida's southernmost outpost when you can prepare this Caribbean favorite with conch from our own waters?

Seafood Pasta Salad

Serves 6 to 8

8 ounces macaroni shells
½ pound salmon fillet
¼ pound scallops
½ Bermuda onion, thin wedges
4 tablespoons Parmesan cheese
¼ pound cooked shrimp, sliced down the middle
¼ pound lobster meat, cut in small pieces (about ½-inch across)
1 cup vegetables, julienned and lightly steamed. Broccoli, carrots, celery, green and red peppers are all good in this salad.

10 black olives, sliced
1 tablespoon parsley, chopped
1 scallion, sliced fine
1 tomato, thin wedges

For the vinaigrette:

1 cup oil
¾ cup vinegar
1 teaspoon basil
1 teaspoon oregano

1 clove garlic, chopped
2 tablespoons sugar
Dash of Tabasco
Salt and fresh black pepper to taste

Cook the pasta until it is *al dente*, then drain and cool.

Steam the salmon and scallops in a small, covered saute pan with a half cup of water for ten minutes, then check the thickest part of the salmon to be sure it is cooked. The flesh should be light in color and should flake easily with a fork. Drain off the water and lift the fish and scallops out, leaving the skin in the pan.

Check the salmon for bones and remove them before breaking the fish into bite-sized chunks. If the scallops are large, you may want to cut them into quarters. Put the fish, pasta, vegetables and other ingredients into a glass dish. Refrigerate while making the vinaigrette.

In a small bowl, mix together all ingredients for the vinaigrette, except the oil. Add the oil in a slow, steady stream, whisking continuously until it is blended well.

Pour the vinaigrette over the salad, stirring it carefully. Cover and refrigerate at least two hours, stirring two or three times to distribute the dressing evenly. Serve chilled.

Calamari Salad

Serves 6 as an appetizer, or 4 as an entrée
2 pounds cleaned squid (See *Kitchen Hints*.)

For the poaching liquid:
2 quarts of water   1 lemon, thin rings
10 whole black peppercorns   2 cloves of garlic, peeled & crushed

For the dressing:
¼ cup tarragon vinegar   1 clove of garlic, minced
1 tablespoon parsely, chopped   1 teaspoon of salt
Dash of white pepper   ¾ cup olive oil

For the final presentation:
1 cucumber, peeled, halved, seeded & sliced
1 cup mushrooms, quartered

Place the water, lemon rings, peppercorns and garlic cloves in a large saucepan and bring it to a boil. Reduce to a simmer and add the squid, stirring to separate. Squid will turn a whitish-pink color and should be done after forty-five seconds to a minute. Drain immediately in a colander and rinse well under cold water to stop the cooking. Spread the cooked calamari in a shallow dish, then remove the peppercorns, lemons and garlic. Refrigerate the squid until it is well-chilled.

In a small bowl, combine the vinegar, garlic, parsley, salt and pepper. Whisk in the olive oil until the dressing is well-blended.

Place the calamari in a salad bowl with half the cucumber and mushrooms. Whisk the dressing and pour two-thirds of it over the combined ingredients. Mix well and season to taste. Put the remaining cucumbers and mushrooms into the small bowl with the dressing. Stir to coat the vegetables evenly. Refrigerate and marinate for at least an hour.

Before serving, arrange the cucumbers and mushrooms on top then garnish with parsley sprigs and thin slices of lemon.

Chilled Poached Halibut
with Dijon Sauce

Chilled seafood is a delight in the summertime! The taste is refreshing, and it's easy on the cook. Poached halibut can be prepared in the morning, then either served as a picnic lunch, or dressed-up and offered at a more formal evening meal.

Allow ½ pound of halibut per person

For the poaching liquid:

3 cups of water	10 black peppercorns
1 small bay leaf	2 lemons sliced into wedges

In a ten-inch frying pan, combine the water, black peppercorns, bay leaf and lemon wedges (give them a little squeeze then drop them in). Bring the water to a boil and add the halibut. The fish must be cooked gently to keep it tender and moist. Maintain a temperature just below the boiling point, cover the pan and simmer for ten minutes. To check for doneness, pierce the fish at the thickest part. If the flesh is opaque throughout, the fish is cooked and can be lifted out of the water with a slotted spoon or spatula. Place the fish on a plate, cover it loosely, and refrigerate it.

For each serving, use two tablespoons each of Dijon mustard and mayonnaise. Mix together well and chill.

When the fish is completely chilled, remove the skin and bones carefully, then arrange the pieces on a platter or individual plates. The sauce can be served in a small dish set on the side of the plate. Garnish with lemon and parsley.

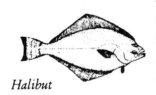

Halibut

Oriental Steamed Salmon

For each person, allow:
½ pound Atlantic salmon fillet
1 tablespoon each of carrot, ginger, and scallion cut into matchstick
pieces 1-inch long.
¼ cup each of teriyaki sauce and water

Cut the salmon into portions and place them in a frying pan of appropriate size. Top each piece with a mixture of the vegetables. In a measuring cup, mix equal parts teriyaki sauce and water, then pour into the pan, cover, and begin cooking over medium heat. Simmer gently for ten minutes, then check for doneness. (See *Kitchen Notes*.)

Remove the salmon carefully. Set each serving in a pool of the sauce on a small, warmed plate. Serve with a side dish of steaming rice.

Blackened Salmon

With the acrid smoke from this cooking, you need a good ventilation system, or prepare it outdoors. In either case, avoid inhaling the smoke.

Allow ½ pound of Atlantic salmon steak or fillet per person
Pan-blackening spice (available at most supermarkets)

To prepare the meal indoors:

Preheat a cast-iron frying pan for ten minutes on the stovetop, using the highest possible heat. Also preheat the oven to 400 degrees.

Coat both sides of the fish with pan-blackening spice. This mix is very spicy, so you'll probably prefer just a light sprinkle on your fish. For the full dose, spread the spices on a plate and lay the fish in them.

Put the fish into the pan and cook for three minutes on each side. Remove from the heat and check for doneness. (See *Kitchen Notes*.) If the salmon needs more cooking, you may wish to finish it in the oven.

To prepare the meal outdoors:

Cook the seasoned fish on a hot grill for about five minutes per side, then check for doneness. (See *Kitchen Notes*.)

Striped Bass in Filo
with Red Pepper Mayonnaise

Roasting the red pepper is best done on a gas flame or outside grill. To willfully char food goes against the grain of most reasonable cooks, yet we ask you to bear with us on this one because the resulting taste simply can't be beat!

Allow ½ pound of bass per person

For the mayonnaise:

1 egg yolk	1 teaspoon lemon juice
¼ teaspoonsalt	Dash white pepper
Roasted red pepper	1 cup salad oil

Using a long handled fork, hold a red bell pepper over an open flame and thoroughly char the outer skin. Once it is all black, enclose it in an airtight container or plastic bag for an hour. Take the pepper out of the bag, immerse it in cold water, and rub the outer, blackened skin to remove it. Cut it in half to remove the seeds and membranes, then cut into medium chunks.

Put all the ingredients for the mayonnaise, except the oil, into a blender or food processor and process until the peppers are puréed. With the blender turned on, add the oil in a slow, steady stream, pausing once to scrape down the sides of the bowl. When the mixture looks like a light pink mayonnaise, it is done, and may be removed to a small bowl and refrigerated until needed.

Check the fish for bones by running your fingers lightly over the surface. Because bass bones usually are large and stubborn, you will probably need a pair of small pliers to remove them. Remove the skin and cut the fish into portion sizes. Refrigerate until needed.

Preheat the oven to 350 degrees.

Carefully unfold the filo dough onto a clean work space. Keep a clean, dampened kitchen towel handy to lay over the unused sheets in case you are interrupted, or they start to dry out while you are working. Peel off a sheet, lay it on the counter and brush it lightly with melted butter. Lay another sheet on top, brush and repeat.

Cut the three sheets in half widthwise. Set a piece of fish (skin-side down) on the filo, about three inches from the end of the rectangle. Lift that three-inch edge up to the fish and roll the dough and fish over once.

Pick up the flaps of dough on either side of the fish and fold them onto what is now the top.

Continue rolling the fish and dough, end over end, keeping the sides tucked in, until you run out of dough.

Place the packet seam-side down onto a buttered cookie sheet, making sure that the edges are tucked in. Ideally, the fish itself will be skin-side down. If not, try to adjust the original placement of the next piece onto the filo.

Wrap each piece of fish, then brush lightly with butter as you place them on the pan.

Bake for twenty to twenty-five minutes. Serve with a generous dollop of the red pepper mayonnaise on the side.

Grilled Swordfish

Serves 4

Allow ½ pound of swordfish per person

To help retain the natural juices in swordfish and to keep it from sticking to the grill, lightly spread each side of the fish with mayonnaise. Depending on the intensity of heat, as well as the thickness of the fish, cook the swordfish for about five minutes on each side. To test for doneness, insert a thin, sharp knife into the flesh at the thickest point. If it meets with any resistance, the fish needs to cook longer. If the knife goes in like butter, the fish is done.

Summer Entrée

*Sometimes, the simplest
is
also the best.
Fresh summer swordfish,
cooked on the grill,
is truly
one of life's
great pleasures.*

Seafood en Brochette

Serves 4

Brochettes take a little time to assemble and should marinate for at least two hours. Once the preparation is complete, however, they are very easy to cook and serve.

For the brochettes:
    1½ pounds of swordfish
    ¾ pound medium raw shrimp, shell-on
    ½ pound medium sea scallops
    16 medium mushrooms
    8 cherry tomatoes
    1 green pepper, cut into chunks
    2 medium Bermuda onions, each cut in 8 wedges

For the marinade: *

½ cup red wine vinegar	½ teaspoon basil
½ teaspoon oregano	1 teaspoon sugar
¼ teaspoon salt	¼ teaspoon black pepper
½ cup ketchup	1 cup oil

In a small bowl, mix together all the ingredients except the oil. Add the oil in a slow, steady stream, stirring with a wire whisk until all of it is incorporated. Set aside until needed.

Peel and devein the shrimp. (See *Kitchen Notes.*) Using a small sharp knife, remove the skin from the swordfish. Cut the fish into 1½-inch squares, keeping in mind that you want to end up with sixteen equal pieces. Quickly rinse the scallops under running water. Drain them and place in a small bowl.

Set up a work area to assemble the brochettes. Within easy reach you will need eight skewers, a 9 X 13 X 2 non-metal baking dish, the vegetables, and the seafood.

Begin each skewer with a pepper chunk, (this allows for easy removal), followed by a piece of swordfish, mushroom, a shrimp, onion wedge, then a scallop. Repeat the sequence, ending with a cherry tomato. In this manner, assemble each, laying them in the baking dish as you go.

Re-mix the marinade, then pour it slowly over the length of each brochette so they all benefit from the seasonings. If you run out of marinade before you have covered all the brochettes, simply tip the dish toward one corner and ladle the juices that have collected there.

Cover the dish and refrigerate for two hours, going back to it several times to re-distribute the marinade as previously described.

These can be cooked under the broiler, but they are really best done on the outside grill. In either case, they should cook about five minutes on each side or until the edges of the swordfish are lightly browned. If some areas of your grill are hotter than others, you may need to re-arrange the skewers periodically.

Serve on a bed of rice and enjoy!

If you would rather not make your own marinade, you can use a commercially prepared salad dressing. We particularly like Ken's Caesar Salad and Zesty Italian dressings.

Note: Once a marinade has been used for raw fish it must be discarded. Do not attempt to serve it, or save leftovers for another meal.

Grilled Yellowfin Tuna
with Tomato Mint Sauce

Allow ½ pound of fresh tuna per person

For the sauce:

1 shallot, diced fine
¼ cup Rose's lime juice
2 tablespoons olive oil
Salt and pepper to taste

½ clove garlic, diced fine
2 tablespoons fresh mint, chopped
2 cups crushed tomatoes

Make the sauce at least two hours ahead to let the flavors mingle. Mix all the ingredients together in a small bowl and refrigerate.

You may wish to remove the skin before cooking. This can easily be done by grasping an edge of the skin firmly in one hand and running a small sharp knife between it and the flesh. Quickly rinse under running water to get rid of any scales on the meat. At this point you can either cook your tuna steak in one piece, or divide it into portions.

Cook over a medium flame for five to seven minutes per side, then test to see if it is done. Insert a small, sharp knife into the thickest part of the fish. If it goes through easily, the fish is done. If it is still dense and tough in the center, it needs to cook longer.

The cold sauce may be served on top, or in a separate side dish.

Grilled Fresh Tuna
with Rosemary Lime Marinade

Allow ½ pound of fresh tuna per person

For the marinade:
2 teaspoons fresh rosemary, stems removed, chopped fine
2 teaspoons garlic, diced fine
½ cup of Rose's lime juice
1 cup olive oil
¼ teaspoon white pepper
½ teaspoon salt

In a small bowl, mix all the ingredients, except the oil. Slowly add the oil in a steady stream, whisking continuously, until it is blended well.

Prepare the tuna by removing the skin as described in the previous recipe. Rinse quickly, pat dry, and cut to portion size. Place the pieces in a glass bowl and pour the marinade over them, turning the fish so that all sides can be exposed to the marinade. Cover and refrigerate for at least two hours, turning occasionally to redistribute juices.

When you are ready to cook, take the fish out of the marinade and let it drain for a minute to prevent flare-ups from excess oil.

Grill the tuna for five to seven minutes on each side. Test for doneness by inserting a small, sharp knife into the thickest part. If the fish is not cooked, it will be firm and dense in the middle. If the knife goes through easily, your dinner is ready!

Note: Once a marinade has been used for raw fish it must be discarded. Do not attempt to serve it, or save leftovers for another meal.

Bluefin tuna

Grilled Striped Bass
with Fresh Fruit Salsa

...ruit salsas are a wonderful new concept. They make a
...w cholesterol alternative to rich sauces, and they taste great!
...lsa can be made with fruits as they are available. Plums,
...ctarines and pears are all appropriate and may be used alone or
...tions. If you choose purple plums, you may want to add
...pers as a color contrast. This is a very colorful dish, giving the
...ace to be creative and dazzle the family or guests!

Allow ½ pound of bass per person

For 2½ cups of fruit salsa:

2 cups of diced fruit	1 tablespoon lime juice
2 tablespoons fresh cilantro	Drizzle of olive oil
1 tablespoon Bermuda onion	1 tablespoon tequila (optional)
3 fresh jalapeño peppers, seeded & diced	Salt to taste

Toss all the salsa ingredients together in a glass bowl. The salsa may
be served immediately or refrigerated to allow the flavors to blend.

Brush both sides of the fish lightly with oil to keep them from
sticking to the grill. Cook for five minutes per side, then test with a fork.
If fish flakes easily at the thickest part, it is done. If not, continue cooking
for two minutes on each side; check again for doneness.

Serve the fruit salsa cold on top of grilled bass.

Mako Shark Steak au Poivre

For 4 servings, allow:
 2 pounds of mako steaks ½- to ¾-inch thick
 3 ounces margarine or butter
 Fresh ground black pepper for dredging the fish

For the sauce:
 1 clove of garlic, diced fine
 4 scallions, cut in ¼-inch slices
 ½ teaspoon salt
 ¾ cup dry white wine

Preheat the oven to 400 degrees.

Cover both sides of the shark steak with freshly ground pepper. You may want a light sprinkle, or you can coat both sides completely. In a ten-inch skillet, melt the butter. Lay the fish into the pan, cover, and cook on medium heat for 4 minutes on each side. At this point, test the fish for doneness by inserting a sharp knife or skewer into the flesh at the thickest part. If it is cooked, the skewer will go through without meeting any resistance. If it is not done, it will feel dense in the center and will need another minute or two on each side. When it is cooked, remove the fish to an heat-proof serving platter and put it into the oven while you finish the sauce.

Toss the garlic into the hot frying pan and cook briefly before adding the wine. Once the wine has been added, shake the pan a few times to loosen the flavorful bits clinging to the sides and bottom. Add the salt and the scallions, swirling the pan a few times to mix them in. A rich, dark brown color, the sauce should be poured onto the fish and served almost immediately after the scallions are added. This will ensure that the scallions keep their vibrant color and that the butter doesn't separate from the sauce to give it an oily appearance and taste.

Menu

Appetizers
Smoked Bluefish Paté
Broiled Oysters on the Half Shell
Oysters Rockefeller
Cape Scallop Appetizer

Soups
Creamy Oyster & Spinach Stew
Cape Scallop Stew

Entrées
Mussels Steamed with Garlic & Wine
Broiled Cape Scallops
Flounder Pinwheels with Mushroom Marsala Sauce
Mussels Palermo
Baked Fish with Pesto
Lobster Pie
Sole Almondine

FALL

The Autumn Catch

Autumn is our favorite season. While spring brings renewal; summer, the beach; and winter, peace and quiet, fall is the sweetest season of all.

Picture this. The days are warm, and the nights are cool. The ocean is even warmer than the air, and that air is crystal clear without a trace of haze or humidity. The crowds are gone, and the locals have money in the bank. Traffic has declined by 75%, and the fishing is unbelievable.

Is there any nicer season than autumn on Cape Cod, Nantucket & Martha's Vineyard? Is there any more beautiful place to be in September, October, and November? Anywhere in New England? In the world?

Swan River hardly shows up on most maps of Cape Cod. When it does appear on nautical charts of Nantucket Sound, it might also be called Swan Pond River, because of the kettle pond that serves as its headwaters. As with all of the rivers and creeks along this coast, this is not a tributary emptying into the Sound, but an estuary, whose currents and depths always ebb and flow, as well as rise and fall with the tides.

As the gull flies, the distance from Swan Pond to Nantucket Sound is only three miles or so; however, all of Swan River's lazy meanderings beneath the bridges, through the tidal wetlands, and beside the backyard docks cause its actual length to be two or three times longer. Because of that, Swan River has long been home to an encyclopedia of sea life.

I remember making coffee some fifteen years ago for a team of divers directed by our Natural Resources Department in the Town of Dennis. They surveyed the oyster population in Swan River from our fish market at Lower County Road north to the next bridge at Route 28, maybe a two-mile stretch. When they were done, they reached the conclusion that the river was home to some 60,000 *bushels* of oysters, ranging in size from spat and immature oysters up to those of harvest-size. They also found an abundance of other shellfish, including quahogs, steamers, whelks, crabs and periwinkles, as well as a wide range of finfish.

Just last fall I was mesmerized by an everyday sight which made work difficult. Each time I looked out the window, I could see striped bass jumping right out of the water. Not just one or two, mind you, but dozens and dozens up and down the river. After two or three days, I just couldn't resist the call, so out came the kayak. For the next few days, I was only available by long distance call; that is, people had to shout out from the banks of the river, and I would try to answer their questions. And all I did was drift with the current and flow between leaping bass, though I would occasionally hook one up just for the fun of it.

As you might expect, I couldn't help but reflect on all those poor people whose work kept them cooped-up in offices and cities. Unfortunately, they had no idea. On days like those you wish for time to stand still and for life to last forever. Clearly, there is no nicer season than autumn on our peninsula and islands.

And, oh yes, the fish.

The Atlantic reaches its warmest temperature in August. And though September brings cooler weather, the aquatic life is at its zenith. Giant bluefin tuna abound off Chatham and on up Stellwagen Bank. The biggest bluefish and striped bass of the season are fattening-up for their migration south. Though not for long, swordfish are still in our waters, and even lobsters are more abundant. The fall run can be the most productive period of the season, and this is truly a time to be thankful, well before Thanksgiving. Change is definitely in the air.

Autumn brings to our fish market two of the most anticipated seasonal delicacies: Wellfleet oysters and Cape bay scallops. Both have been the subjects of books on their own, and both deserve them.

Wives tales of old have it that oysters should only be eaten during months with an *R* in them. That season runs from September to April. While that tale is not true, oysters in the fall and winter do have a decidedly better consistency and flavor. They spawn in the warmer months, so they often are found to be watery and bland. As the water cools, however, oysters become much more appealing, firm and white. Of course, if you must have an oyster in July or August, those coldwater Wellfleets, as well as those from Cotuit, will still satisfy.

At Swan River we have had the same folks from Wellfleet bringing them to us for over twenty years. Woody and Peggy are as knowledgeable about oysters as any people I know. They have made oysters their life. They harvest both wild and farmed oysters from their own grant, and they have seen entire crops of oysters destroyed by mysterious aquatic

Oyster

diseases. They've suffered storm damage from hurricanes and nor'easters, but they keep on oystering. And if Wellfleet has any oysters to harvest at all, Woody and Peggy arrive at the market, smiling away.

There are many ways to eat oysters, all satisfying. But the *absolute* finest is simply the way nature prepares them. Raw and *au natural*. I've even "tested" them from a digger with my morning coffee. Their flavor is so delicate and unique, that no condiment does it justice.

The true art to opening oysters is also lost on too many people. A properly-shucked oyster should be opened carefully enough so that the oyster's meat remains intact, not cut. (Please see *Kitchen Notes*.) The opened oyster also should never be rinsed with freshwater. The *liquor* within the oyster holds much of the flavor and saltiness.

Cape bay scallops are the second seafood treat that arrives in the fall. The season opens on different days throughout the Cape & Islands, but it creates as much anticipation and excitement around here as deer-hunting season does elsewhere. Everyone wants to know: Which towns have good harvests? Which got shut out? Where will the action be this year?

The effect of a good scallop season will be felt throughout a town all winter long. Unfortunately, the good years are becoming more rare. Chatham hasn't seen a good year for at least five years. Dennis had an extraordinary harvest only four years ago, possibly the best ever. Since then, however, there has been no real harvest. Without a doubt, 1993 proved to be the worst year I have ever seen for Cape scallop production.

Meanwhile, we were fortunate to have one Nantucket fisherman selling to us all winter long. A great many people do not realize that the island is the richest scallop fishery along the entire eastern seaboard, and he was one of only a handful of watermen working through the unforgettably severe winter months that ran from '93 into '94. Via small airplane, he actually flew us his catch of forty pounds a day.

Bay scallops have become a generic term for small scallops from all over the world: Chinese bays, Peruvian bays, Icelandic bays, Mexican bays, and Carolina bays, just to name a few. The average price for these imported bays is $2 per pound; however, we paid our island fisherman $9.50 to $10 per pound all winter long, and that should say all that must be said about the difference between these products.

Unfortunately, summer visitors to the Cape & Islands never get to experience the taste of fresh Cape scallops. There really is no comparison to any other scallop. Certainly, ours must have a high natural sugar content, because they are the sweetest things you'll ever eat that isn't a dessert! Often out on the boat we would eat them right from the shell.

Local bay scallops are wonderful eating in any preparation. We enjoy them deep-fried, in stews, in stir-fries, in Newburgs, or in casseroles. The possibilities are really endless, but the first scallops of the season are always cooked the same simple way in our house. Place them in a baking dish, sprinkle with unseasoned breadcrumbs, put a few pats of butter on top, and broil for about five minutes. Let the great taste of the scallops provide the seasoning. There really is nothing like it.

Harvesting scallops was one of the greatest thrills of my fishing adventures. If the Scallop Gods permit, they are found in bays and rivers close to shore throughout the Cape & Islands. Often we would be fishing in little coves and channels well-protected from rough seas. The process consists of towing two to four 100-pound dredges along the bay bottom until they are full of whatever is down there. We would simply stop the boat, pull the dredges on board, and cull through the contents.

Of course, once you had your limit and you headed for shore, your day was only half over. You still had to shuck your catch, which remains a mind-numbing process. Back then, our legal limit was twenty bushels per day, with each bushel containing hundreds of scallops. I still remember being so tired by the end of the day that we would virtually be rocking back and forth as though we were still on the boat. We'd check with each other, "My boat's rocking. How 'bout yours?" Some nights we would finish shucking our catch at ten or eleven at night, only to be rising again at five the next morning to head out in the boat once more.

Fortunately, the various towns usually don't allow commercial scalloping on Sundays, and I have never known any relaxation like those Sundays during scallop season. The days of a fisherman remain much like that on a year-round basis, and I have tremendous respect for their work ethic. For all the bad press that the fishing industry has received because of overfishing, I would love to see one of their armchair critics try to keep up with a fisherman's pace for a week.

The other day, I read an interesting article in an industry magazine called *Seafood Leader*. "Fishermen harvest what they're allowed to harvest," wrote Roger Fitzgerald. "Catching as many fish as they can is how they make their living. Regulating them is how [fishery] managers make theirs. If a stock is depleted, it's not because of greedy fishermen: it's because of mismanagement. Period." I think that puts it perfectly. Don't blame fishermen for catching too many fish. Only twenty years ago the government was encouraging fishermen to build bigger and better boats in order to catch more fish.

But I digress.

Let's eat!

The Autumn Catch

If the Scallop Gods permit, scallops can be found in bays and rivers throughout Cape Cod, Nantucket & Martha's Vineyard.

Smoked Bluefish Paté

Yields about 1½ cups

This paté is quite versatile. Served with crackers, it can be either molded into a shape on a plate, or put into a crock. Using a star attachment on a pastry bag, you could pipe the paté onto Melba toast or cucumber slices and garnish with fresh dill.

½ pound smoked bluefish	1½ teaspoons lemon juice
4 ounces cream cheese	1 teaspoon fresh dill, chopped
1½ teaspoons horseradish	¼ cup light cream

Remove skin and break-up the bluefish, checking carefully for bones. Put the fish, plus the remaining ingredients (except the cream) into a blender or food processor. Stopping at least once to scrape down the sides of the bowl, blend until everything is chopped well. With the machine still running, add the cream in a steady stream. Process for a minute or two, stopping when the mixture is a smooth paste.

Broiled Oysters on the Half Shell

Serves 4

24 oysters	Breadcrumbs
Tabasco	Butter
Lemon juice	

Preheat the oven to 400 degrees.

Shuck the oysters (See *Kitchen Notes*), but save the bottom shells. They are shaped like shallow bowls and hold the juice quite nicely during cooking. If available, rock salt makes a great bed for cooking oysters. It stabilizes the shells in the oven, holds the heat, and provides an elegant look that can be taken to the table or buffet.

Arrange oysters in their half shells on a broiling pan. Add to each: a dash of Tabasco, a few drops of lemon juice, a sprinkle of breadcrumbs and a small pat of butter. Place the tray about six inches beneath the broiler and cook briefly until the crumbs are lightly browned, and the edges of the oysters begin to curl. Serve hot with narrow wedges of lemon.

Oysters Rockefeller

Serves 6

3 dozen opened oysters on the half shell
4 tablespoons butter or margarine   3/4 cup of breadcrumbs
½ cup onion, diced fine   2 tablespoons Pernod
1 package frozen spinach   Salt and pepper to taste

Defrost the spinach, then chop and squeeze it to remove excess liquid. Sauté the onions in the butter until they are golden brown. Remove them from the heat and add the Pernod. Return to heat and reduce the liquid slightly by cooking for another minute. Put the onions and their juices into a bowl and mix in the spinach, breadcrumbs, salt and pepper.

Arrange the opened oysters in a shallow baking dish (on a bed of rock salt if it is available.) Place two tablespoons of stuffing on each oyster.

(At this point, they may be refrigerated to cook later.)

Bake in a preheated, 400-degree oven for about ten minutes or until the topping browns. Keep in mind that they will take longer to cook if they have been in the refrigerator.

Cape Scallop Appetizer

While Dijon mustard and chutney might appear to make an unseemly combination, this is a wonderful taste treat! Serve on scallop shells with a parsley garnish.

For each person, allow:

3 to 4 ounces of bay scallops   1 tablespoon chutney
1 tablespoon Dijon mustard   2 teaspoons butter

In a sauté pan of appropriate size, melt the butter, then add the scallops and cook on medium heat for five minutes. Stir in the mustard and chutney, then continue cooking until it is heated through.

Serve immediately.

Bay scallop

Creamy Oyster & Spinach Stew

Serves 4 to 6

1 pint fresh oysters, shucked and in their juice
1 12-ounce package frozen leaf spinach,
    or use half of a 10-ounce pack of fresh spinach
6 tablespoons butter or margarine
6 tablespoons flour
2 cups of fish stock (See *Kitchen Notes.*)
2 cups of light cream or milk
Pinch of white pepper
Pinch of nutmeg

Frozen spinach should be thawed, squeezed dry, and chopped; fresh spinach should have stems and tough leaves removed, then be rinsed and steamed until limp before it is chopped.

Melt four tablespoons of the butter in a four-quart saucepan. Add the flour and cook together on medium heat, stirring frequently for about five minutes. Slowly add in the fish stock, stirring with a wire whisk until the mixture is smooth. Add the milk in the same manner and continue stirring for a few minutes as it thickens. Add the spinach and seasonings. Reduce the heat to low and stir periodically while preparing the oysters.

In a medium frying pan, melt two tablespoons of butter and add the oysters. Cook on medium heat just until the edges of the oysters begin to curl. Combine cooked oysters and their juices with the cream mixture. Heat well and serve.

Note: Oyster stew does not want to wait to be served. Once it is hot, it will curdle easily, and the oysters will quickly overcook.

Cape Scallop Stew

For each person, allow:

4 to 6 ounces of Cape scallops
1 small pat of butter
1 tablespoon shallots, chopped fine
1 cup cream or milk
Salt and pepper to taste

Heat the cream slowly while preparing the scallops.

In a frying pan of appropriate size, melt the butter, add the shallots, and cook on medium heat for a few minutes until the shallots are tender and clear. Add the scallops and cook for about five minutes, tossing the pan lightly once or twice to ensure even cooking. Look for the scallops to firm up slightly and give off a milky liquid. At this point, add the hot cream, salt and pepper. Leave the stew on the heat until it is piping hot, remembering that scallops take very little time to cook to perfection.

Spoon the stew into bowls and serve, adding a few finely sliced scallions or a sprinkle of paprika to garnish.

Autumn Soup

This is the way most Cape fishermen eat their scallops!

Mussels Steamed with Garlic & Wine

Serves 8 as an appetizer, 6 as a lunch, or 4 as a dinner

6 pounds of mussels (See *Kitchen Notes.*)
4 cloves of garlic, chopped fine
1 tablespoon fresh parsley, chopped
½ cup white wine
½ cup butter or margarine
½ cup water

In a small saucepan, melt the butter, add the garlic and cook gently for five minutes. Add the wine, water, and parsley. Heat the mixture for five more minutes, and it is ready to use.

Place the mussels into a large pan, such as a six-quart Dutch oven. Pour the broth over them and cook on medium to high heat. Once the mussels have come to a boil and a good head of steam has developed, reduce the heat slightly so that the broth doesn't boil over. Steam the mussels for five to ten minutes or until all the shells are opened.

Serve in large shallow bowls with the broth and plenty of crisp French bread for dipping.

Broiled Cape Scallops

Serves 4

Every time I plan to cook Cape scallops at home, I go over possible recipes and methods of preparation. I keep telling myself that I really should try something new and different; however, nine times out of ten this is how I prepare them. "It's so simple and delicious," I reason, "why mess with perfection?"

    1½ pounds scallops
    ¼ cup melted butter or margarine
    ½ cup breadcrumbs
    2 scallions (optional)
    Salt and pepper to taste

Preheat the broiler.

Place the scallops in a shallow baking dish suitable for broiling. They should be packed closely together, but not piled upon each other. Pour the melted butter over the top and sprinkle with breadcrumbs. Cook under the broiler, not too close to the heat, for about ten minutes. (Sometimes I will mix in a few finely-sliced scallions midway through the cooking. This gives me a chance to check their progress and to add a little subtle flavor.) The crumbs should be golden brown, and the scallop meats themselves should be solid white throughout.

Cape scallops are so tender that it is easy to be fooled as to whether or not they are cooked. Don't worry about undercooking them, though, because scallops can be eaten raw!

Flounder Pinwheels
with Mushroom Marsala Sauce

Serves 4

This dish can be prepared up to a day in advance; just pop it in the oven when you're ready.

2 pounds medium flounder fillets, somewhat uniform in size.

For the pinwheels:

1 package of frozen spinach, chopped
¼ cup sweet red pepper, diced fine
6 to 8 ounces Swiss cheese, sliced thin
2 shallots, diced fine

For the sauce:

1 cup sliced mushrooms
3 tablespoons butter or margarine
4 tablespoons flour
1½ cups fish stock, heated (See *Kitchen Notes.*)
¼ cup Marsala
Salt and pepper to taste

Melt the butter in a medium sauté pan, add the mushrooms and cook for five minutes, tossing the pan lightly to ensure even cooking. Add the flour and continue cooking, stirring until the flour is no longer visible. Combine the fish stock and Marsala, then slowly pour it into the mushroom/flour mix, stirring with a wire whisk to prevent lumps from forming. Add salt and pepper to taste, then simmer for five to ten minutes, stirring periodically, until thickened. Set aside.

To prepare the pinwheels:

Defrost the spinach and squeeze out the excess moisture. Mix together in a bowl the spinach, the red peppers, and the shallots. Lay a piece of fish upon a clean work surface, skin-side up.* Cover the fillet with a slice of cheese, then a thin layer of the spinach mix.

Beginning with the thin end of the fillet, roll the fish. Holding both sides firmly, cut down through the center of the roll with a very sharp knife. Place these two sections, cut-side up, in a shallow baking dish. It takes a little manipulating to keep the pinwheels upright and tightly-rolled and you may wish to use toothpicks to keep them in line. Just be sure to remove them after baking.

At this point you could cover and refrigerate the fish and sauce separately, or you could proceed to the next phase of preparation.

To prepare the meal:

Heat the sauce while the fish is cooking.

Preheat the oven to 400 degrees.

Put a half cup of water in the pan with the fish, cover tightly with foil, and bake for ten to fifteen minutes. If you are using a glass dish, or if the preparation has been kept in the refrigerator for any period of time, you may need to cook a little longer. In any case, check for doneness by taking a peek inside one of the rolls. The cheese should be melted, and the fish should flake easily with a fork.

To present the meal:

When the fish comes out of the oven you may wish to strain the juices from the baking dish into the sauce. It is not completely necessary, but it will add to the flavor. Rest a mesh strainer over the sauce pot. Holding the fish back with a spatula, gently tip the baking dish so that the juices can run out of one corner, through the strainer and into the sauce. Blend in the juices, then ladle about a quarter-inch layer of sauce onto a heated platter or individual dinner plates. Place the pinwheels on the sauce and serve. Extra sauce can be served in a separate dish.

While the fish will not have the skin on it, the skin side can be differentiated by silvery patches and slightly darker coloration.

Autumn Entrée

This Swan River original looks great and tastes even better. Use it when you want to show off.

Mussels Palermo

Makes a first course for 6, or a hearty entrée for 4

Once you get past the chopping of vegetables and cleaning of mussels, this tasty concoction can be put together quickly. If you are short of time at the dinner hour, you can do the prep earlier in the day, put the ingredients into little bowls on a tray in the refrigerator, then toss it all together like a pro at the appointed hour.

6 pounds mussels in the shell (See *Kitchen Notes*.)	
4 tablespoon olive oil	½ cup Marsala
20 whole black olives	12 pepperoncini, ½-inch sections,
4 cloves of garlic, diced	stems removed
1 cup mushrooms, quartered	½ teaspoon salt
1 cup cherry tomatoes, quartered	Fresh ground black pepper
1 cup leeks, in ½-inch slices	Linguine for 4 people (as entrée)

When you are ready to put the meal together, cook the linguine according to package directions. Cook the pasta *al dente*, because it will be heated again and could easily overcook.

In a ten-inch to twelve-inch skillet heat the oil, add the garlic, and cook briefly. Next add the rinsed leeks and mushrooms, tossing the pan a few times to coat everything with oil. Cook over medium heat for five minutes, stirring frequently. Once the white ends of the leeks are clear, add the cherry tomatoes, pepperoncini, olives, seasonings and Marsala. Cover and simmer gently for five minutes, then test a leek to be sure it is tender throughout.

Once the leeks are cooked, add in the cooked mussel meats and hot linguine. Cook another five minutes until it is piping hot.

Two notes of caution may be needed. First, this dish is best when the vegetables are just cooked, because overcooking causes them to loose their shape and color. Second, once the mussels have been added, either stir carefully, or shake the pan so that you don't break up the mussel meats.

Using a spaghetti lifter, take out the pasta first, then ladle the rest over top. Have Parmesan cheese and a peppermill available on the table.

Baked Fish with Pesto

Frequently in the early fall, we are inundated with fresh basil. What better use is there for basil than to make pesto? And what better use is there for pesto than spread upon a fresh piece of fish for baking?

Many types of fish qualify for this special treatment. We have used tilefish with wonderful results, as well as whiting, ocean catfish, and monkfish. Even shellfish, such as shrimp and scallops, succumb to the charms of pesto. Select the best from the fish counter and you will be on your way to a fine meal.

For each person, allow:
  ½ pound of fish

For the pesto:
  1 cup of fresh basil   ½ cup olive oil
  2 cloves of garlic, diced   ¾ cup Parmesan cheese
  ½ cup walnuts   ¼ teaspoon fresh black pepper

This recipe yields a very flavorful mixture, so a thin layer on top of the fish is all you will need. If there is any left over, it can be kept in the refrigerator or freezer for another use.

Remove the coarse stems of the basil, as well as any shriveled leaves, rinse, then pack well into the cup for measurement. Place all the ingredients into a food processor, and blend until it forms a smooth paste, stopping once or twice to scrape down the sides of the bowl.

Preheat the oven to 400 degrees.

Put the fish into a shallow baking dish, spread the pesto on top and bake, allowing ten minutes per inch measured through the thickest part of the fish. Test with a fork or sharp knife for doneness. The fish should be opaque throughout and flake easily.

Whiting

Lobster Pie

Serves 4 to 6

1 to 1½ pounds of lobster

For the biscuit crust:

2 cups of flour	3 tablespoons butter
4 teaspoons of baking powder	1 teaspoon tarragon
½ teaspoon of salt	1 cup milk or light cream
1 tablespoon sugar	

For the sauce:

4 tablespoons flour	1 tablespoon sherry
4 tablespoons butter	½ cup grated cheddar cheese
1 tablespoon shallots, diced fine	½ teaspoon tarragon
1 cup whole milk or light cream	1 teaspoon Dijon mustard
1 cup fish stock (See *Kitchen Notes*.)	Pinch of white pepper

To prepare the biscuits:

Mix the dry ingredients. Cut in the butter until the mixture resembles coarse corn meal, then stir in the milk. Mix only until blended together, then turn the dough onto a floured board or countertop. Roll the dough to a ¾-inch thickness and cut into round shapes, four inches in diameter.

To prepare the sauce:

Melt the butter in a small saucepan. Add the shallots and cook, stirring for four or five minutes. Add the flour, stir, and cook for about five more minutes on medium heat. Blend the sherry into the stock, then pour this mixture slowly into the pan, stirring constantly with a wire whisk. When the stock is hot and blended, add the remaining items. Reduce heat and cook, stirring frequently, until sauce is hot and thickened. Add salt to taste, remembering that commercial bouillon has quite a bit of salt. Set the sauce aside while you prepare the lobster meat.

To make the pie:

Preheat the oven to 375 degrees.

Remove any cartilage and veins from the lobster meat, then cut into bite-sized pieces. Place the meat into a shallow baking dish and cover with sauce. Arrange the biscuits on top. Bake for twenty minutes or until the crust is golden brown, and the edges of the lobster sauce are bubbling.

Sole Almondine

Serves 4

In the seafood world, there is nothing as delicate as the taste of fresh sole. Add to it the sweet, nutty flavor of buttered almonds, and you have a combination that is sure to please the most discriminating palate!

2 pounds fresh sole fillet
½ cup almonds, sliced (not slivered)
¼ butter or margarine
1 tablespoon lemon juice
Pinch of salt

Begin by melting the butter with the salt and lemon juice. Put the almonds into a bowl and pour the butter mix over them, stirring to coat the almonds.

Preheat the over to 400 degrees.

Using melted butter or margarine, brush the bottom of a shallow baking dish and lay the fillets (skin-side* down) into it. Top each piece with almonds and bake for ten minutes, or until the almonds are golden brown and the fish flakes easily with a fork. Using a long metal spatula, carefully transfer the fish to warm dinner plates and serve.

The fish will not actually have the skin on it, but we put this side down anyway for cosmetic reasons. The skin side can be determined by silvery traces and slightly darker coloration.

Menu

Appetizers
Portuguese Stuffed Mussels
Shrimp & Artichoke Hearts Wrapped with Bacon
Crabmeat Patrice
Terry's Clams Casino
Smoked Salmon & Caviar Pizza

Soups
Spicy Seafood Stew
New England Fish Chowder

Entrées
Scrod Oreganata
Baked Fish with Breadcrumbs & Fennel Seeds
Baked Fish with Cheddar Crumbs
Newburg Sauce
Seafood Newburg en Casserole
Sea Scallops Marsala
Mussels Marinara
Sea Scallops Provençal

WINTER

The Winter Catch

Winter brings many changes to the waters of Cape Cod, Nantucket & Martha's Vineyard. Lobstermen from Menemsha on the western edge of the Vineyard to Provincetown at the outermost tip of the Cape all bring in their traps for the winter. The weirs are pulled and stacked on Hardings Beach in Chatham. Rods and reels used for bluefish and striped bass are in basements for overhauling. Even the floating docks which fill the harbors like Wychmere in Harwichport and Great Harbor in Nantucket are pulled out of the water. Winter rules, and Cape & Islands fishermen have learned how to cope.

Still, fishing does not come to a halt.

This past winter we couldn't count the number of days the cod fishing boats had to break ice in the harbors to get out to fish. When we wanted to check to see if any boats were out we would only have to look for broken ice, and we would know. On windy days, the large boats that managed to get out would have one person in charge of just breaking ice off the boat's riggings with a hatchet. Because the ice makes it top-heavy, a boat covered with frozen sea spray easily can capsize.

As bad as all that sounds, there is nothing like the pride on a fisherman's face when he comes home with a good catch in the face of that adversity. In fact, rarely do we hear any fisherman complain about the weather in winter. About the wind, maybe; about a lack of fish, definitely; but *never* about the temperature. Sometimes they report that the temperature is warmer on the ocean than it is on land. The ocean might drop to thirty-four degrees Fahrenheit, creating a warming effect on a day in the teens.

Shellfishing also continues in winter. Clam flats are workable unless covered with ice. Most towns set temperature minimums to protect young shellfish from freezing. If the air temperature drops below 30 degrees, the diggers have to just watch and wait. Don't tell the warden, but we have known fishermen to turn their thermometers toward the sun to help boost it a few precious degrees. I often chuckle at how people will say how cold it looks on the water, when they are sitting in their cars with the heat on high. Those fishermen out in the elements are often sweating from the exertion of clamming. I have done it, raking for clams out in Stage Harbor, back to the wind, eyes watering from the cold. But if your waders are watertight, and your long-johns are dry, you really don't mind the weather. And that hot coffee surely works when you hit the shore!

Another offshore fishery that thrives in winter is sea scalloping. Cape Cod Bay produces some great sea scallops in the winter. Large and tender, these are high quality scallops. Rave as we do about bay scallops, dayboat sea scallops can be equally as good, though different in taste. Some people actually like them better, because they are not as sweet.

The key to a good sea scallop has always been the length of time that a boat is out to sea. The large boats from New Bedford, Gloucester, and elsewhere are out catching scallops for seven to ten days per trip. Those scallops are often old before they even hit the dock. Mainly out of ports on the North side of the Cape, only a few local boats get involved in this activity. Provincetown, Wellfleet, Orleans, Dennis, Barnstable and Sandwich all have harbors that might see landings of sea scallops, and these smallboat scallopers working out of our ports are out for a maximum of twenty-four hours. So, the quality of their catch is terrific.

Unfortunately, another "miracle" has recently affected scallop quality. It is a chemical approved by the Food and Drug Administration to treat scallops with freshwater. While the purpose of this soaking is to add weight to the scallops, it also preserves them, giving them a greater shelf-life. That means that processors can take a hundred pounds of scallops, add the chemical, soak them overnight, and legally have one hundred and twenty-five pounds of scallops for sale! Of course, they have to post a sign stating that these are "Scallop product, 25% water added."

Guess how often that happens. How many restaurant diners see *Scallop product newburg* on the menu? But how many diners have noticed scallops just don't taste the way that they used to? Or that there is a funny aftertaste, a little burn on their tongue after eating scallops. Please don't stop eating scallops. Just be sure to ask if they are processed or *dry*. *Dry scallops* are the new lingo for *real scallops*, the way they always were: natural and fresh from the sea!

Scallops are also the only shellfish to have a patron saint. St. James,

The key to a good sea scallop has always been the length of time that a boat is out to sea.

the apostle, wore scallop shells as his emblem. Pilgrims who visited his shrine during the Middle Ages wore the shells in tribute to him. The famous scallop dish, *Coquille Saint-Jacques*, takes its name from him.

Winter also brings an added advantage to Cape & Islands seafood as the quality of our local fish reaches its pinnacle for the year. The simple reason for this is that Mother Nature acts like a refrigerator, keeping the fisherman's catch cold through every phase of its journey to us. While our own fishermen always bring ice on their boats to help preserve the quality of their catch, this is not the case with all fishermen. So, winter weather helps to maintain quality of all the fish that is landed throughout Cape Cod, Nantucket & Martha's Vineyard, and the shelf-life of fresh fish increases by two or three days when the weather is frosty.

This is also very true of shellfish. Mussels, for example, only stay alive for two or three days in the summer. The warm weather actually decreases oxygen levels of inshore waters. Mussels taken in winter live for five or six days. Shellfish also are much fuller in the winter. Just as the locals do, they fatten-up in the winter. (Not enough exercise, I guess.) Twelve quahogs shucked in winter yields one pint of meat, while twelve quahogs shucked in summer yields about three-quarters of a pint.

Pollution along inshore waters is also significantly lessened in the winter. With our population reduced, there is less stress on the eco-system throughout the Cape & Islands. Quality just can't be surpassed in winter.

The biggest problem, though, is that we do see many days in winter when fishing is just plain impossible. Fishermen never plan vacations. The wind will do that for them. In fact, the fishermen are more in touch with the weather than anyone else I know. Farmers are affected by it. People who work outdoors are affected by it. But fishermen are really in touch with it. They listen to broadcasts from the National Oceanic and Atmospheric Administration (NOAA) throughout the day on marine frequencies, and they know from wind direction whether to expect rain or sunshine. If you want to know tomorrow's weather, you're far better off asking a fisherman than a weatherman. The outdoors is their office! Fishermen can read clouds and wave-chops and wind speeds the way most businesspeople read faxes and financial reports. Fishermen commune with the natural world, much like our Native American predecessors. In the winter, more than the rest of the year, that is a matter of life and death.

Winter is also chowder season. Somehow the thought of a thick, creamy chowder just doesn't work for you when you're in someplace like Florida. Or Phoenix. Or California. But when you're chilled to the bone, and it's damp and raw outside, there are few more welcoming thoughts than a tasty clam or fish chowder waiting for you inside.

While there are dozens (if not hundreds) of recipes out there for chowder, there are but a handful of key rules that any *good* chowder must follow. Good fresh fish and/or clams certainly are near the top of that list. Fresh spuds are also important. But the Number One Rule for a great chowder is plenty of onion!

Start with butter or margarine or oil or lard or pork rind. Whatever. And use fish stock or clam juice. Whatever. But you must plan on plenty of onion sautéed first. *That* is the flavor binder, the key to a good chowder. If you're going to be stingy with the onion, then you might just as well open up a can of soup!

There is also good news for chowder lovers who are watching their fat levels. Cecy has developed a wonderful recipe for a dairy-free clam chowder that delivers all the flavor and creamy texture of a good chowder, while it remains a lot kinder on the cardiovascular system.

Winter is definitely a season of beauty throughout the Cape & Islands. Most people who visit here do so in the warm weather. Their images of this peninsula and islands are shaped by summertime activities, and they are wonderful; however, the real Cape Cod, the real Nantucket, the real Martha's Vineyard are far easier to find during winter than in any other season.

Portuguese Stuffed Mussels

Yields 50 stuffed mussels

Though this is a somewhat time-consuming recipe, it can easily be broken down into manageable segments. For example, the first two steps could be done on one day, then the assembling could be finished the next day. In addition, you can always freeze the completed stuffed mussels and have them ready to bake as needed.

3 pounds mussels in their shell (See *Kitchen Notes.*)

2 cups bread bits	2 plum tomatoes
2 tablespoons olive oil	3 ounces chourico (Portuguese
1 tablespoon garlic, chopped fine	hot sausage)
4 tablespoons butter or margarine	¼ teaspoon red pepper
½ cup onion, diced ¼-inch cubes	1 tablespoon parsley, chopped
1 cup reserved broth from mussels	1 tablespoon cilantro, chopped

In a ten-quart pot, bring one cup of water to a boil and add the mussels. Cover and allow the mussels to steam for six or seven minutes. Check to be sure all the shells are opened. If not, resume cooking until they are. Drain the cooking liquid and reserve for later use.

Once the mussels are cool enough to handle, remove them from their shells, de-beard them and rinse in a large bowl of cold water to wash away any remaining grit. Lift the mussels out of the water and set them in the refrigerator until they are chilled. Cold mussels are firmer, easier to cut, and less likely to break up in the stuffing mix.

Because you will need fifty half shells to stuff, sort through the shells and select enough mid-sized ones. Rinse well and refrigerate until needed.

To make the bread bits:

The object here is not to create breadcrumbs, but pieces the size of a commercial stuffing mix.

Preheat the oven to 350 degrees.

Take a six-inch segment of Italian bread (stale is fine), tear it into pieces, then put them on a cookie pan to bake. After five minutes, remove them from the oven, break down the larger pieces, and repeat until all the bread is crispy and reduced to very coarse crumbs.

To prepare the stuffing:

Heat a ten-inch skillet, then add the oil and butter. Once the butter is melted, add the onion and garlic, cooking on a medium heat until the onions are clear. Remove seeds and pulp from the tomatoes, then cut into a quarter-inch dice. Add the tomatoes and the chourico to the onions, then cook for a few minutes. Pour one cup of the reserved broth into the skillet. Simmer this mix gently for ten minutes to allow the flavors to mix.

Lay the cooled mussel meats in a row upon a cutting board and cut them with a long, sharp knife. The pieces should be about the size of a large pea. After the initial pass of the knife down the row of mussels, go back and re-cut those that may have been cut lengthwise. Be careful not to *overcut*, or you will soon have a rather unappetizing mess in front of you.

Add the herbs into the simmering pot, stir briefly, then add the mussels.

Put the bread bits into a large bowl and add the mussel mix, stirring carefully, just until all the ingredients are combined. Let the mixture cool for ten minutes, then stuff the shells with one tablespoon of stuffing mix in each.

Preheat the oven to 400 degrees. Bake for five or six minutes, or until the mussels are lightly-browned on top. Avoid overcooking so that they do not dry out.

Winter Appetizer

Despite the effort, this appetizer is well worth it!

Shrimp & Artichoke Hearts Wrapped with Bacon

These make wonderful hors d'oeuvres for holiday entertaining. If you wish, you can make them a day ahead, then bake as needed.

Allow 4 or 5 medium shrimp per person
1 package of frozen artichoke hearts
Bacon strips, partially-cooked and cut in half

Preheat the oven to 400 degrees.

Thaw the artichoke hearts and cut lengthwise into quarters. Fold the shrimp around the artichoke heart, wrap with bacon and secure with a toothpick. Place in a shallow baking dish and bake until the bacon is crisp. They will probably take a total of ten minutes, but should be checked and turned over after five minutes.

Crabmeat Patrice

Another fine addition to your repertoire of holiday appetizers!

8 ounces cream cheese (room temperature)
6 to 8 ounces crabmeat   ¼ teaspoon salt
1 tablespoon milk   Dash of white pepper
½ teaspoon horseradish   ¼ cup almonds, sliced

Preheat the oven to 375 degrees.

Combine everything together except the almonds, then spread the mixture in a small, shallow baking dish. Sprinkle the almonds on top and bake for fifteen minutes.

Serve hot or cold with Melba toast, crackers, or crudites.

Terry's Clams Casino

Serves 6

Thanks to Terry Shepherd for this refreshing recipe.

36 littleneck clams, rinsed well
1 clove of garlic, diced fine
1 small onion, diced into ¼-inch pieces
½ green pepper, diced fine
5 strips of bacon, cut into 1-inch pieces

Mix together the cut vegetables in a small bowl and set aside. Open the clams, free the meat from the bottom shell, and place them on the half shell in a shallow dish suitable for broiling. Place about one tablespoon of the stuffing on each clam, then top with bacon.

Cook them under the broiler until the bacon is crisp and brown.

Smoked Salmon & Caviar Pizza

An appetizer for 6 to 8, or an elegant lunch for 4

For the pizza dough and crust:

See *Gourmet Pizza with White Clam Sauce* on page 20.

For the topping:

¼ pound smoked salmon (either lox or dry-smoked salmon)
8 ounces Boursin herbed cheese
2 tablespoons caviar

Make and bake the pizza dough according to the instructions on page 20.

Preheat the oven to 350 degrees.

Spread the Boursin onto the cooked pizza crust. Cut the smoked fish into small slices and place on top of the cheese. Heat the pizza for ten minutes. Dot the top of the pizza with caviar, then transfer to a serving platter, cut, and serve.

Spicy Seafood Stew

Serves 4 to 6

This recipe evolved as a means of using the little packets of leftover seafood that always seemed to accumulate in our freezer. A few shrimp scampi, a lobster tail, and some scrod were the basis of our first version, but your own may vary according to the ingredients available to you. If you choose to follow the recipe below, but raw clams or mussels are not used, you may substitute bottled clam juice or seafood bouillion cubes for the broth.

2 tablespoons olive oil	8 littleneck clams, rinsed well
2 cloves garlic, chopped fine	8 small mussels, scrubbed and
1 onion, diced	de-bearded (See *Kitchen Notes.*)
1 medium potato, diced	¼ pound shrimp, shelled and
1 stalk celery, diced	deveined
1 medium carrot, diced	¼ pound scallops
1 leek, cut into ½-inch lengths	½ pound firm white fish
1 teaspoon thyme	¼ teaspoon black pepper
1 tablespoon flour	Dash of white pepper
1 15-ounce can tomato sauce	¼ teaspoon crushed red pepper
2 tablespoons lime juice	1 tablespoon parsley, chopped

Steam the mussels and clams in a medium saucepan using a half cup of water. Drain off the broth and set aside. Allow the shellfish to cool, then remove the meats from shells and reserve.

In a small saucepan cook the carrot and potato together in one cup of water. When the vegetables are cooked *al dente*, drain the cooking liquid into the container with the shellfish broth and set both the liquid and the vegetables aside.

Heat a large pot and add the oil. Cook the garlic, onion, celery, and leek on medium heat, stirring occasionally, until the onions are clear. Sprinkle the flour into the pot and cook, stirring for three or four minutes until it is mixed-in well. Add the liquids reserved from the shellfish and vegetables. Stir well to ensure that the flour blends in without making lumps, then add all of the remaining ingredients *except* the fish and shellfish. Simmer for twenty minutes, then add in the seafood. From that point, the stew will need to cook another fifteen minutes; however, it should not go too much longer as the fish could easily overcook.

New England Fish Chowder

Serves 4

For this hearty cream soup choose a firm white fish, such as ocean catfish, monkfish, haddock, halibut, or cod.

5 slices of bacon, in ¼-inch pieces	3 tablespoons flour
½ cup onion, diced	3 cups whole milk or cream
¼ cup celery, diced	¼ teaspoon thyme
1½ pounds white fish	2 tablespoons oil, margarine, or
1½ pounds potatoes diced	the bacon drippings

Remove skin and bones from the fish and rinse. In a medium-sized skillet, bring one cup of water to a boil and add the thyme. Lay the fish in the water, cover, and simmer gently for seven to ten minutes. When the fish has cooked, drain and reserve the broth to use in the chowder.

Dice the potatoes into half-inch cubes and cook in a small saucepan with one cup of water. When the potatoes are tender, drain the water into the fish broth, then set it and the potatoes aside.

In a four-quart saucepan, cook the bacon until crisp and remove from the pan with a slotted spoon. Either using the bacon drippings, or two tablespoons of oil or margarine, sauté the onions and celery until tender.

Add the flour into the pan with the onions and celery and cook for a few minutes on medium heat, stirring to prevent scorching. Slowly add in the broth mixture, stirring with a wire whisk to work out lumps. Allow this to cook for a few minutes, then add the milk and stir to blend.

Add in the potatoes, the bacon and the fish, then heat the chowder until it is piping hot. Once the fish and potatoes have been added, stir very gently to prevent the fish from breaking apart. Also, be careful not to let the chowder become so hot that the milk will curdle.

Though the chowder is now ready to serve, many locals feel it is better the second day. If you can wait that long, allow it to cool, then refrigerate until the next day.

Haddock

Scrod Oreganata

Serves 4

2 pounds of fish

For the crumb mix:

1 cup seasoned breadcrumbs	1 teaspoon basil
½ cup Parmesan cheese	¼ teaspoon salt
1 teaspoon oregano	¼ teaspoon black pepper

Preheat the oven to 400 degrees.

Combine the dry ingredients to make crumb mix. Remove skin from fish (see *Kitchen Notes.*), rinse quickly in cold, running water, cut into portion sizes, and pat dry with a paper towel. Lightly coat fish with oil or melted butter. Sprinkle both sides of fish generously with crumbs and place in shallow baking dish.

Bake for ten to twelve minutes. Check the thickest part of the fillet to be sure it is cooked through. Serve immediately.

Baked Fish
with Breadcrumbs & Fennel Seeds

Serves 4

2 pounds of white fish	Salt and pepper to taste
¼ cup melted butter	1 teaspoon fennel seeds
1 tablespoon lemon juice	½ cup breadcrumbs

Preheat oven to 400 degrees.

Place the fish fillet in a shallow baking dish. Drizzle with melted butter, to which the lemon juice has been added. Salt and pepper to taste. Crush the fennel seeds with mortar and pestle. Sprinkle the fennel onto the fish, then coat lightly with breadcrumbs.

Bake ten to fifteen minutes, depending on the thickness of the fish. Test with a fork in the thickest part of the fish to see if it is done. If the flesh flakes easily and is white throughout, it is ready to serve. If it is still translucent in the center, cook it for another five minutes, then test again.

Baked Fish with Cheddar Crumbs

Serves 4

An easy preparation, even the kids may like this one!

2 pounds of white fish

½ cup *Better Cheddar* crackers, crushed
¼ cup breadcrumbs
¼ cup Parmesan cheese
2 tablespoons melted butter or margarine

Preheat the oven to 350 degrees.
Mix together the crumbs, cheese, and melted butter, then sprinkle
generously on the fillets. Bake for fifteen minutes or until fish can be
flaked with a fork.

*These
three recipes
are all appropriate
for many white fish,
including:
scrod, whiting, hake,
ocean catfish, haddock,
or halibut.*

Newburg Sauce

Serves 2

Newburg sauce can be used in a variety of ways with seafood. An enduring favorite is a casserole of mixed fish and shellfish, topped with sauce, baked, then served with toast points. The sauce can be used as a topping for any broiled fish, combined with shrimp or lobster for an elegant entree, or used with crepes for a luncheon. Regardless of how you choose to use it, this sauce creates a hearty winter dish.

1 tablespoon butter or margarine	1 cup light cream
2 tablespoons flour	½ teaspoon Worcestershire sauce
2 tablespoons sherry	2 to 3 drops Tabasco
1 teaspoon paprika	Dash of salt

Melt the butter in a small saucepan. Add the flour and cook, stirring frequently, for three minutes. In a small bowl, combine the sherry, paprika, Worcestershire sauce, Tabasco, and salt. Add this mixture into the melted butter and flour, stirring with a wire whisk to blend. Almost immediately, add the cream in a slow steady stream, whisking at the same time to prevent lumps from forming. Continue stirring over medium heat until sauce thickens, then reduce heat to a very low temperature and cook for another five minutes.

The sauce is now ready to serve, or to be refrigerated until needed.

Seafood Newburg en Casserole

This recipe serves 6 people, but it can easily be multiplied to feed a crowd.

1½ pounds of scrod or other white fish
½ pound scallops
½ pound uncooked shrimp, peeled and deveined
6 ounces lobster meat
Double recipe of Newburg sauce

Arrange the fish, scallops, and shrimp in a nine-by-twelve-inch baking dish. Pour a half cup of water into the pan and cover it with a lid or foil. Bake for twenty to thirty minutes. Check for doneness by flaking the fish with a fork or by cutting into a scallop to be sure it is white throughout.

When the fish is fully-cooked, carefully drain the cooking juice, and save it to add to the sauce.

Remove the cartilage and sand vein from the lobster meat, cut into bite-size pieces, then arrange on top of the other fish.

Stir the fish broth into the sauce, then pour it over the fish mixture so that it covers the seafood well. This may be baked immediately or refrigerated until needed.

If you are cooking it directly, the casserole will need about fifteen to twenty minutes (uncovered) in a 375-degree oven. If it has been held in the refrigerator, it should be ready after about thirty minutes. In either case, it is ready when the center is hot, and the edges are bubbling.

You may wish to add toast points just before serving, or have them available on the side. In any case...*Bon Appétit!*

Sea Scallops Marsala

Serves 4

Here is a quick and easy preparation for scallops!

1½ to 2 pounds of scallops
½ cup Marsala   Black pepper to taste
¼ cup melted butter   Swiss cheese to cover scallops
¼ cup breadcrumbs

Preheat the oven to 400 degrees.

Arrange the scallops in shallow baking dish so that they fit either in a single layer, or no deeper than two layers. Drizzle the Marsala over them according to taste. Follow with a little melted butter, freshly ground black pepper, and a layer of Swiss cheese. Sprinkle the top with a dusting of bread crumbs. Bake for fifteen to twenty minutes, or until the edges are bubbling, and the top is a light golden color.

Mussels Marinara

Serves 4 to 6

In my family there are two schools of thought on the subject of mussels in a sauce such as this. My husband thinks the mussels should be cooked *in* the sauce, *in* their shells, and served over linguine, *just like that!* His argument is that the flavor produced by such a method should not be sacrificed for tidiness. While his view has certain merits, I still maintain that shells *in* a tomato sauce are a messy affair and may try the patience of some diners.

As a domestic compromise, I offer both versions of the recipe so that you may decide which method suits you according to the delicacy or gusto of the people you will be feeding.

4 tablespoons olive oil	½ teaspoon oregano
½ cup onion, chopped	½ teaspoon basil
½ cup green pepper, chopped	10 black olives, sliced
½ cup mushrooms, sliced	1 15-ounce can tomato sauce
2 cloves garlic, diced fine	¼ cup red wine
4 pounds mussels in their shells	Salt and pepper to taste
(See *Kitchen Notes*.)	Linguine

In a large skillet, sauté all the vegetables in the olive oil until they are tender and the onions are clear. Add in the remaining ingredients (*except* the mussels) and simmer gently for about fifteen minutes. Add in the mussels, either uncooked *in* the shell, or cooked *out* of the shell. If you have chosen to use the mussels in the shell, cook for about fifteen minutes or until the shells open. If you have chosen to use the pre-cooked mussels removed from the shell, cook only five or ten minutes in the hot sauce.

Prepare the pasta according to directions on package.

Pour the sauce over steaming hot spaghetti or linguine and serve... with plenty of napkins!

Sea Scallops Provençal

Serves 4

1½ to 2 pounds of scallops

For the breading mix:
¾ cup breadcrumbs
¾ cup flour
¼ cup Parmesan cheese
2 tablespoons parsley, chopped

For the garlic butter mix:
¼ cup butter
4 tablespoons white wine
2 teaspoons garlic, chopped fine

Preheat the oven to 400 degrees.

Mix the breading ingredients in a spacious bowl. Add the scallops and toss until they are completely coated. Lift the scallops out of the crumb mix and place them in a baking dish in a single, snug layer. Sprinkle a little of the crumb mix on top of the scallops, then drizzle with the garlic butter.

Bake for fifteen to twenty minutes. To check for doneness, cut into one of the scallops to be sure it is opaque in the center. Be careful not to overcook them, or they will become tough and dry.

Notes

Determining Freshness
Storing Seafood ❖ Freezing Seafood ❖ Defrosting Seafood
Preparing Seafood for Cooking ❖ Skinning Finfish
Cooking Fish ❖ Checking for Doneness
Making Fish Stock
About Mussels
Inspecting Mussels ❖ Cleaning Mussels ❖ Steaming Mussels
Opening Oysters
Peeling Shrimp ❖ Deveining Shrimp
Cleaning Squid

KITCHEN NOTES

Determining Freshness

Selecting seafood can be a bewildering experience for the uninitiated. If you buy from a reputable fish market, it is perfectly acceptable to ask your fish dealer's recommendation. Ask what the dealer would take home that night. On the other hand, if you have a certain type of fish in mind, you would like to be able to see for yourself that it is fresh.

In general, the fillets of the white fish (such as, cod haddock, sole, ocean catfish, cusk, etc.) should have a pearly white appearance and firm-looking flesh. Others, such as pollock and flounder have a slightly grayer appearance which should be translucent. If you can see the fish whole, look for bright red gills and clear eyes (as opposed to foggy, sunken ones). Avoid fillets that are yellowing, dry looking, or crusty on the outer edges. Above all, fresh fish should not have a strong odor. Remember, "If it smells like fish, it's bait!"

Storing Seafood

Because they are highly perishable, fish and shellfish need to be kept as cold as possible. When you get the fish home, you should keep it in the coldest part of your refrigerator and remember to return the fish to the refrigerator between any stages of preparation.

If you need to keep the fish for more than a day or two, itransfer it to a plastic, rather than paper wrap. Lobsters are the exception here. Though they should be kept in a paper bag, you should not store them longer than a day. And no matter what your well-intentioned friends might say, *never* attempt to keep lobsters alive in water. They are saltwater creatures that need very cold, aerated water.

Freezing Seafood

When it becomes necessary or desirable to freeze seafood, it is worth following a few simple procedures to prevent freezer-burn. A serious hazard that affects the quality of frozen fish, freezer-burn occurs when the seafood is exposed to the drying effects of the freezer atmosphere.

To keep the frigid air away from uncooked fish, we give it a protective coating of lightly-salted water. To make your own solution, dissolve a half teaspoon of salt into one cup of water.

If you are freezing scallops, put them into an appropriate-sized plastic container, cover them with the salted water, then jostle the container once or twice so the water will travel down into the air spaces.

Freezing uncooked fillets utilizes the same principal. Place the fillet flat inside a plastic bag. Keeping the bottom of the bag on the counter, pour in just enough water to surround the fish. Starting at the end with the fish in it, fold the bag over a few times, then lay it on a flat baking dish in such a way the water will not flow out.

If you need to freeze more than one piece of fish, divide them into serving sizes and freeze each in a separate bag. Set the bags on a baking sheet to freeze, then remove the frozen blocks and store them in a more convenient way in the freezer. It is best to keep the packets in a single layer so they don't freeze together.

When defrosting anything frozen in salted water, always discard the water and give the fish a quick rinse. It goes without saying that a person on a sodium-restricted diet would not choose this method of freezing.

Though cooked lobster meat does freeze well in the salt solution, *cooked* seafood generally fares better when tightly encased in plastic wrap. Leftovers that will be used in soups or stews can be stored in plastic containers and covered with a bit of fish stock or clam juice.

Remember to label and date the food you keep in the freezer.

Defrosting Seafood

Obviously, it is preferable to use fresh fish exclusively; however, that is not always possible. To maintain the quality of any frozen seafood, care must be taken to defrost it correctly. The best method is to move the item from the freezer to the refrigerator twenty-four hours before needed. If you have the foresight to do this, simply place the frozen item in a pan to collect any water that may result from the thawing, and you are all set.

For the 98% of us, who will not usually be planning the meal that far in advance, more drastic measures must be employed. In this case, the preferred method would be to place the fish into a sturdy plastic bag, then immerse it in cold water. For best results, use a lot of water and force the bag under the water by putting a weight of some sort on top. Be aware of two important things. One is that most fish readily absorb fresh water and should never be soaked unless in a bag. The other is that warm or hot water must never be used, because it encourages the rapid proliferation of the bacteria naturally present in any fish or shellfish.

A possible exception to using a plastic bag would be when defrosting squid or shrimp in the shell. If you need only a few squid or shrimp from a large frozen block, set the block in a colander under cold running water until you are able to break away as many as you need.

While a microwave can be used to defrost fish, be careful not to actually cook some areas while leaving others frozen. The microwave can be used effectively if you set the timer for very short increments, then turn, re-arrange, and break down the frozen mass as you go along.

If you have a pint of chopped clams, for example, set the timer for forty-five seconds just to loosen the clams from their original container. Then turn the semi-frozen lump into a low flat bowl and microwave it another forty-five seconds. At this point, you may be able to cut the whole thing into four segments, microwave it again, and so on until the clams are loose enough to use, yet not cooked. This method works well with frozen cooked lobster or crabmeat, but not for uncooked shrimp.

Preparing Seafood for Cooking

It is always a good idea to inspect your finfish for bones before you cook it. This can be done by carefully running your finger along the length of the fillet, down the center of the non-skin side. Even if the skin is not on the fish, it is easy to tell which is the *skin* side by the silvery-gray tone left when the skin was removed. There may also be bones up near the nape of the flatfish (flounder and sole). Again, these can be located with a light touch of the fingers. The bones can usually be removed easily by hand, but in some cases you may need to use a small pair of pliers. Bones are rarely found in the larger fish, such as bass and tuna, but you will definitely need pliers to pull any out.

When preparing crabmeat or oyster dishes, be on the look-out for bits of shell, which can be picked-out manually..

Scallops should be checked for bits of shell or grit. These tiny inedible contaminants can be dealt with quite easily. For each pound of scallops, mix two teaspoons of salt with four cups of water in a medium-sized bowl. Add the scallops and move them around in the water so that the grit and shells fall to the bottom of the dish. Carefully lift the scallops and drain them in a colander. This same method can be used for cooked or raw, shucked clams, as well as cooked, shucked mussels.

It is said that fresh water is the enemy of dead fish. Any time you feel it is necessary to rinse fish, it would be a good idea to mix up a solution of one teaspoon salt to two cups cold water, dip the fish quickly, then drain it in a strainer or pat it dry with paper towels.

Skinning Finfish

If a recipe calls for *skinned* fish, you can request it of the fish market, or you can skin it yourself without much difficulty.

Lay the fillet flat on a cutting board, close to the edge of the counter. Holding the tail end firmly with your left hand, begin at the tail end to cut into the flesh: first directing the blade toward the skin side, then laying it at an angle almost parallel to the cutting board. Hold the knife at this angle and simultaneously begin making sawing motions back and forth while pulling the skin piece off to the left. The knife should stay almost parallel to the cutting board, while the skin is being pulled along, separating it from the flesh of the fish. With practice, this skill will become easier, enabling you to remove the skin from any fillet.

In the case of larger fish, such as swordfish, tuna, and halibut, the skin can most easily be removed after the fish is cooked. Simply take a sharp knife and run it around the edge of the steak, separating the skin from the meat. The same applies to *uncooked* large fish, but the bond between the skin and flesh is just a little stronger and requires more effort to remove.

Cooking Fish

In general, fish cooks very quickly. In the oven, on the grill, or in a saute pan, the same rule of thumb applies: allow ten minutes cooking for each inch of thickness. If you have added any stuffing to the basic fillet, you will need to adjust the time. Be aware, however, that it is far easier to overcook than undercook your fish. Even after the seafood has been removed from the direct source of heat, some cooking may continue. So, you must carefully time the actual cooking and test for doneness.

Checking for Doneness

There are a several ways to check your fish to be sure it is cooked through. The most reliable method is to actually look into it. Each fish will have a slightly different texture, but this method can be used reliably for everything from sole to scallops to swordfish. Insert a small sharp knife into the fish at the thickest point and check the flesh there. If it is done, the flesh will be opaque, and the meat will flake easily where it has been disturbed by the knife. If the fish is not done, the interior will be a translucent gray, and the flesh will feel firm and somewhat gummy.

A quick way to check the larger fish, (swordfish, shark, tuna, etc.) is to pierce it with a skewer or a small sharp knife. This works especially well if you are cooking on the grill and the light is not strong enough for a visual check. If the fish is cooked, the skewer will go through the thickest part as though it were butter. If the fish is not quite done, the skewer will meet resistance, and you have to cook it a little longer. To get the feeling for *doneness* using this method, first check a thin section of the fish, then go to a thicker part. You should feel the difference right away.

Since there are always a variety of factors that influence cooking time, I am usually reluctant to prescribe exact cooking times. When people ask me how long to cook fish, I have to respond: "Until it's done!"

Making Fish Stock

Though commercial stocks and bouillion cubes are readily available in supermarkets, keep in mind that they might be saltier than this one. This stock can be made anytime and frozen in one-pint containers.

1 medium fish frame (from a 4- or 5-pound cod, haddock or pollock)
1 onion, quartered
2 stalks of celery, cut in chunks
1 carrot, cut in chunks

Pinch of thyme
10 black peppercorns
4 sprigs of parsley
1 small bay leaf

Cut the fish frame in two or three pieces so that it will fit into a ten-quart pot. Add the vegetables and herbs, then cover with cold water. Bring the contents almost to a boil and reduce the heat slightly to simmer for about forty minutes. Strain the stock first through a colander, then through a strainer lined with cheesecloth. Pour it into pint containers, allow it to cool, then place it on a flat surface in the freezer.

About Mussels

Mussels are indeed an under-appreciated local treasure! While their popularity is growing in the United States, they have been enjoyed by gourmets in other parts of the world for a long time. Their full hearty flavor and versatility make them a culinary delight for seafood lovers and cooks alike. Though mussels vary in size, they average ten to eighteen per pound, and a serving would be about 1½ pounds (as weighed in the shell).

Inspecting Mussels

Mussels do require a little extra care in handling, however, and we must be diligent about inspecting and cleaning them. Mussels tend to gape or open even shortly after being taken from the water. If you pinch a mussel's two shells together, and they close up again (however slowly), the mussel is alive and fine to use. On the other hand, if the mussel doesn't respond, it is dead and must be discarded.

The mussels whose shells are held together tightly must also be scrutinized carefully, because some of them may be full of mud. To let a *mudder* get by your inspection is to destroy an entire dish. The damage is usually discovered at the last possible moment when it is too late to make corrections. In the case of closed mussels, the dead ones can be detected by holding each mussel firmly in one hand and attempting to slide one shell over the other, using a slight, twisting motion. If it is a *mudder*, the top shell will slide right off, and a culinary disaster will be avoided.

Cleaning Mussels

Once the preliminary inspection has been completed, and the dead mussels are safely in the garbage bin, you will need to clean the shells of seaweed and the little bits of grit you will likely find. I usually set up a two-part operation in the sink: one pan of water for the wash, and a colander to drain them after. Set the mussels beside your wash water, then dip them one by one into the pan while scrubbing each lightly with a small, stiff brush. This should be enough to clean them, but once in a while you may come across a barnacle that should be removed with a small, sharp knife. (A clam knife is ideal if you have one.) Drain the cleaned mussels in the colander.

Whenever a recipe calls for mussels to be cooked *in the shell*, you need to de-beard them beforehand. Simply use your fingers to pull-off the small clump of tough fibers that the mussel uses to attach itself to rocks. If you will be using only the mussel meats out of the shell, it is easier to remove the beards after they have been steamed.

Steaming Mussels

To steam the mussels, choose an appropriate-sized pan (flat and shallow is better than tall in deep), put about an inch of water in the bottom, cover it, then heat until boiling. Add the mussels and cook for five to ten minutes, or until all the shells are open. Drain the broth (this can be used in your recipe or frozen for use later as a fish stock) and refrigerate the mussels in a shallow pan. When they are cool enough to handle, they can be removed from the shell.

First, pinch the beard between your fingers and pull it away, while you squeeze the two shells gently together to hold the meat in. Next, pull the mussel from the shell and place the meat into a container. Be sure to keep these mussel meats cold until you are ready to use them.

Opening Oysters

Probably the safest method of opening oysters is to use a simple *church key* can opener. First, locate the hinge at the narrow end of the oyster shell, where the top and bottom halves are joined together. Place the oyster on on a stable surface, cover it with a dish towel, then use the pointed end of the church key to pry open the rear hinge. Once you get the oyster to pop open, simply reach in with a paring knife and cut the single muscle that attaches the oyster to both halves of the shell. And *please*, don't cut the oyster meat.

Peeling Shrimp

Shrimp can be peeled and cleaned either by hand, or by using a plastic shrimp peeler. Holding the tail segment firmly with your left hand, use your right hand to peel apart the shell where the back section joins the leg sections. Loosen this back shell by working your way from the tail toward the head end. After all the back shell segments have been removed, pull off the legs. In some cases you may wish to leave the last section and the tail on the shrimp. If not, they can be taken off next.

Deveining Shrimp

To remove the vein, make a shallow cut along the outer, topside of the peeled shrimp and pull out the sand vein. In some cases the vein may be very hard to see. This is not a problem, because it has been flushed clean, and you need not worry about it further.

Cleaning Squid

Before cleaning squid for a recipe, keep in mind that it takes one-and-a-half pounds of uncleaned squid to yield one pound of clean squid.

Begin by separating the tentacles and head from the body. Grabbing the squid gently behind the eyes, pull the tentacles and head out of the body. Be aware of the fact that squid does have a sack of black ink within that you will encounter either at this point, or when you clean the body. Disregarding the innards for the moment, push the tentacles apart so that you can find the mouth at their base. You should be able to feel the *beak* with your fingertip and to remove it with a squeeze between your two thumbnails. Once it pops-up, simply pull the beak out.

Next, make a clean slice between the eyes and the tentacles, then discard the head and the connected innards. Generally, the tentacles are kept as one piece.

Cleaning the body is even easier. Use your fingers to feel inside the body cavity for the clear piece of long, narrow, flat cartilage that looks very much like a piece of plastic. Take it out and throw it away. Finally, remove the thin skin of the squid by first scratching the body with your thumbnail, then peeling away the skin. When you're done, rinse thoroughly. Some recipes will call for the body to be sliced into rings; others, to be kept whole.

Index

— A —

aquaculture 39, 42
Atlantic salmon 27 (*illustration*), 39
– Salmon in Filo w/ Scallion Remoulade 27
– Smoked Salmon Primavera 28
– Seafood Pasta Salad 48
– Oriental Steamed Salmon 51
– Blackened Salmon 51
– Smoked Salmon & Caviar Pizza 87

— B —

Baked Fish w/ Cheddar Crumbs 91
Baked Fish w/ Pesto 74
Barnstable 81
Bass River 16
bay scallops 17, 64, 67 (*illustration*)
– Broiled Cape Scallops 71
big-eye tuna 38
black-back flounder 16
black-tip shark 37
blue crab 45
bluefin tuna 38, 57 (*illustration*)
bluefish 15, 36
– Smoked Bluefish Paté 66
Boston 7, 9, 10, 16
Broiled Cape Scallops 71
Broiled Oysters on the Half Shell 66
bullraking 41

— C —

calamari (see *squid*)
Cape Cod Bay 15, 42

Cape dogfish (see *dogfish*)
Cape bay scallops 17, 64, 67 (*illustration*)
– Cape Scallop Appetizer 67
– Cape Scallop Stew 69
– Broiled Cape Scallops 71
catfish (see *ocean catfish*)
caviar 87
Chatham 7, 10, 16, 18, 38, 42, 64
Chesapeake Bay 17, 19
cherrystones 18, 39
chowder 83
– Dairy-Free Clam Chowder 22
– Key West Conch Chowder 47
– New England Fish Chowder 89
chowder clams 38
clams (see also *cherrystones, chowder clams, littlenecks, quahogs, sea clams, steamers, surf clams*) 14, 18, 41
cod 9 (*illustration*), 10, 11, 16, 38, 43
– Scrod San Sebastian 33
– Baked Fish w/ Pesto 74
– Spicy Seafood Stew 88
– New England Fish Chowder 89
– Scrod Oreganata 90
– Baked Fish w/ Cheddar Crumbs 91
Coe, Franny 40
conch 41
– Key West Conch Chowder 47
Coquille Saint-Jacques 82
Cotuit 63
crab (see also *blue crab, rock crab*) 19, 63
crabmeat 23
– Crabmeat w/ Cocktail Sauce 45
– Crabmeat Spread on Toast Rounds 45
– Crabmeat Patrice 86
Creamy Oyster & Spinach Stew 68
cusk 10

— D —

dab flounder 16
Dairy-Free Clam Chowder 22
Dennis 42, 62, 64, 77
dogfish 37, 38
dolphins 39
dragger 9, 14, 16

— E —

Eastham 42
eel 16, 36
estuary 16, 19, 62

— F —

fettucine 28
filo dough 27, 52
finfish 10, 16, 63
fishermen 7, 8, 9, 37
fishery management 10, 16
fish stock
– making (*Kitchen Notes*) 102
flatfish 11, 16
flounder (see also *black-back, dab, fluke, sole, yellowtail*) 11, 16, 17, 38
– **Flounder Florentine w/ White Cream Sauce** 24
– **Flounder Pinwheels w/ Mushroom Marsala Sauce** 72
fluke 16
fresh fruit salsa 58
Fulton's Fish Market 38

— G —

Georges Bank 9, 10, 16, 38
George's Fish Market 19
Gloucester 10, 81
Gourmet Pizza w/ White Clam Sauce 20
Great Harbor 80
grey sole 16
Gulf of Maine 15, 39

— H —

haddock 9, 11, 38, 43, 89 (*illustration*)
– **New England Fish Chowder** 89
hake 9, 10
halibut 38, 50 (*illustration*)
– **Chilled Poached Halibut with Dijon Sauce** 50
hand-jigging 9
Hardings Beach 80
hardshell clams (see also *quahog*) 17
Harwichport 10, 19, 38, 80
herring 14
Herring River 15
Hollandaise sauce 23
hook-fishing 9, 10
Hoskins, Dot 31
Hynes, Capt. Pat 38

— J —

jigging (see *hand-jigging*)

— K —

Keys (Florida) 37, 41, 47
– **Key West Conch Chowder** 47
king mackerel 37
Kitchen Notes 98-105

— L —

lemon shark 37
lemon sole 16
littleneck clams (see also *quahogs*) 41
– **Shrimp & Clams w/ Linguine** 30
– **Scrod San Sebastian** 33
– **Terry's Clams Casino** 87
– **Spicy Seafood Stew** 88
Linguine w/ White Clam Sauce 32
lobster 36, 42, 43 (*illustration*)
– **Seafood Pasta Salad** 48
– **Lobster Pie** 76
– **Seafood Newburg en Casserole** 92
lobstering 19
Lucas, Captain Paul 15

— M —

mackerel 15
– **Mackerel en Papillote** 25
– **Mackerel w/ Sesame-Dijon Glaze** 27
mako shark 37
– **Mako Shark au Poivre** 59
Mashpee 36
Menemsha 80
Mitchell River 16
monkfish 17

Index

– Baked Fish w/ Pesto 74
Montagna, Cosmo 11
Morris Island 42
mushroom Marsala sauce 72
mussels 39, 41, 42, 82
– **Mussels Diablo** 44
– **Marinated Mussels** 46
– **Mussels Steamed w/ Garlic & Wine** 70
– **Mussels Palermo** 75
– **Portuguese Stuffed Mussels** 84
– **Spicy Seafood Stew** 88
– **Mussels Marinara** 94
– about mussels (*Kitchen Notes*) 102-103

— N —

National Oceanographic & Atmospheric
   Administration (NOAA) 82
New Bedford 10, 16, 81
Newburg sauce 92
New England Fish Chowder 89
North Atlantic 9
Nova Scotia 39

— O —

ocean catfish 10, 11
– **Baked Fish w/ Pesto** 74
offshore 9-11
Orleans 42, 81
overfishing 10, 11
oysters 39, 62, 63 (*illustration*)
– **Broiled Oysters on the Half Shell** 66
– **Oysters Rockefeller** 67
– **Creamy Oyster & Spinach Stew** 68
– opening 104 (*Kitchen Notes*)

— P —

Parkers River 16
pizza dough 20
pesto 74
Pleasant Bay 42
pollock 9, 10, 16
Popponesset Beach 36
porpoises 39
Portuguese Stuffed Mussels 84
primavera
– **Smoked Salmon Primavera** 28
Provincetown 42, 81

— Q —

quahog (see also *cherrystones, hardshell clams,
   littlenecks*) 17, 18, 21 (*illustration*), 39, 41, 63
– **Gourmet Pizza w/ White Clam Sauce** 20
– **Dairy-Free Clam Chowder** 22
– **Shrimp & Clams w/ Linguine** 30
– **Linguine w/ White Clam Sauce** 32

— R —

red pepper mayonnaise 52
rock crab 45 (*illustration*)
rod-and-reel tuna fishing 38
Rosemary lime marinade 57

— S —

salmon (see *Atlantic salmon*)
Salmon in Filo w/ Scallion Remoulade 27
Sandwich 42, 81
sand shark (see also *dogfish*) 37
scallops (see also *bay scallops, Cape scallops,
   sea scallops*) 17, 41, 63, 64
– **Seafood Pasta Salad** 48
– **Seafood en Brochette** 54
– **Cape Scallop Appetizer** 67
– **Cape Scallop Stew** 69
– **Broiled Cape Scallops** 71
– **Baked Fish w/ Pesto** 74
– **Spicy Seafood Stew** 88
– **Seafood Newburg en Casserole** 92
scallion remoulade 27
scrod (see also *cod* and *white fish*) 9, 11
– **Scrod San Sebastian** 33
– **Scrod Oreganata** 90
schrod (see *scrod*)
sea clams 17, 18
– **Gourmet Pizza w/ White Clam Sauce** 20
– **Linguine w/ White Clam Sauce** 32
Seafood Pasta Salad 48
Seafood en Brochette 54
Seafood Newburg en Casserole 92
sea scallops 81
– **Sea Scallops Marsala** 93
– **Sea Scallops Provençal** 95
shad 14
shad roe 14
– **Shad Roe** 31
shark (see also *black-tip, dogfish, lemon, mako,
   sand*) 36
shedders 43
shellfishermen 17, 81

Shepherd, Terry 87
shrimp 30
 − Shrimp & Clams w/ Linguine 30
 − Seafood Pasta Salad 48
 − Seafood en Brochette 54
 − Baked Fish w/ Pesto 74
 − Shrimp & Artichoke Hearts Wrapped w/ Bacon 86
 − Spicy Seafood Stew 88
 − Seafood Newburg en Casserole 92
 − peeling and deveining (Kitchen Notes) 104-105
skinning fish (Kitchen Notes) 101
slammers 16
Smoked Bluefish Paté 66
Smoked Salmon & Caviar Pizza 87
Smoked Salmon Primavera 28
softshell clams (see also steamers) 17
sole (see also flounder, gray sole, lemon sole) 11, 16
 − Sole Oscar 23
 − Sole Almondine 77
Spicy Seafood Stew 88
squid 14, 15 (illustration),
 − Squid Bolognase 29
 − Calamari Salad 49
 − cleaning (Kitchen Notes) 105
Stage Harbor 81
steamers (see also clams) 16, 17, 40, 63
Stellwagen Bank 63
stew
 − Creamy Oyster & Spinach Stew 68
 − Cape Scallop Stew 69
 − Spicy Seafood Stew 88
stock (see fish stock)
striped bass 36, 37 (illustration)
 − Striped Bass in Filo w/ Red Pepper Mayonnaise 52
 − Grilled Striped Bass with Fresh Fruit Salsa 58
Stellwagen Bank 63
stock (see fish stock)
striped bass 37 (illustration)
surf clams (see sea clams)
surimi 19
Swan River 16, 62
swordfish 36
 − Grilled Swordfish (illustration) 53
 − Seafood en Brochette 54

— T —

tilefish 75

toast rounds 29, 45
tomato mint sauce 56
Town Cove 42
trap-fishing 14
trawling (see tub trawling)
tub trawling 9
tuna (see also bluefin, big-eye, yellowfin) 36, 38, 39,
 − Grilled Fresh Tuna w/ Rosemary Lime Marinade 57

— U —

underutilized fish 10

— V —

Vining, George 19

— W —

Wallace, David 42
weirs (see also trap-fishing) 14
Wellfleet 63, 81
whales 39
white clam sauce 20, 32
white fish 9
 − Scrod San Sebastian 33
 − Baked Fish w/ Pesto 74
 − Spicy Seafood Stew 88
 − New England Fish Chowder 89
 − Scrod Oreganata 90
 − Baked Fish w/ Cheddar Crumbs 91
whiting 11, 75 (illustration)
Woodworth, Glen 20
Woody & Peggy 63
Wychmere Harbor 80

— Y —

yellowfin tuna 38
 − Grilled Yellowfin Tuna w/ Tomato Mint Sauce 56
yellowtail flounder 16

Acknowledgments

The true heart and soul of this book can be found in the people who have worked at Swan River Fish Market & Restaurant over the years that we have been here. A seasonal business is a strange animal, and there is no business course available to prepare for such madness. Each year a crew of returnees comes together with a group of new faces to carry on the spirit of years past. Morale always builds, and everyone pulls together to deliver a great product under a great deal of stress.

No one person has set the tone and established the character of Swan River Fish Market over the past twenty years any more than Jim Stone. Unfortunately, Jim passed away only days ago. He was loved by customers and co-workers alike, because he truly cared about people. Kerry Cassin also helped set the standards of quality which we adhere to every day.

Glen Woodworth, our *chef extraordinaire* (and aspiring rock star!), deserves major kudos for juggling dozens of young workers with one hand, while turning-out hundreds of consistently inspired dinners with the other. And he does that all with great humor!

Over the years, the torch has passed to new people as veteran employees guide them along. A special tip of the hat goes to Artie Eaton, Megyen Green, Andy Colby, Sue Warner, Debbie Demetriou, and countless other long-time employees at Swan River.

There have been literally hundreds of others who have toiled with us to put themselves through college or to get started with their lives. We enjoy nothing more than watching these young people come into Swanee at the age of 14 or 15, work and grow over their years here, then return as grown-ups with families of their own. We like to believe that we have helped somehow in our own way to help them in that sometimes difficult growth from teen-agers to adults.

We would like to thank Charlotte Ventola for her help over the years in our own transition from employees to employers.

And we must thank our two fabulous sons, Eric and Brendan. They have had to deal with a lot of competition for their time during the making of this book, as well as the running of Swan River. They are the pride and joy of our lives.

Many others helped test the recipes and re-read these fishtales. They are too numerous to mention, but we thank you all very much.

Finally, we would like to thank Fred Sargent and his wife Brenda. Fred's father, Captain Don Sargent, founded Swan River Fish Market nearly fifty years ago, and Fred worked many years to establish Swan River as the great place that it is. We are forever in his debt for believing in us and allowing us the opportunity to continue what he and his father had started.

Thank you one and all.